WORKING WITH CHILDREN & FAMILIES
AFFECTED BY
SUBSTANCE ABUSE

A Guide for Early Childhood Education and Human Service Staff

KATHLEEN PULLAN WATKINS / LUCIUS DURANT, JR.

**THE CENTER FOR APPLIED
RESEARCH IN EDUCATION**
West Nyack, New York 10994

Library of Congress Cataloging-in-Publication Data

Watkins, Kathleen Pullan
    Working with children and families affected by substance abuse : a guide for early childhood education and human service staff / by Kathleen Pullan Watkins and Lucius Durant, Jr.
       p.   cm.
    Includes bibliographical references.
    ISBN 0-87628-935-9
    1. Problem families—United States.   2. Family social work—United States.   3. Social work with children—United States.   4. Social work with alcoholics—United States.   5. Social work with narcotic addicts—United States.   6. Problem children—Substance use—United States—Prevention.   I. Durant, Lucius, 1932– .   II. Center for Applied Research in Education.   III. Title.
HV699.W38   1996
362.29'13'0973—dc20

96-2494
CIP

© 1996 by The Center for Applied Research in Education West Nyack, New York

Printed in the United States of America

10 9 8 7 6 5 4 3 2 1

ISBN 0-87628-935-9

ATTENTION: CORPORATIONS AND SCHOOLS

The Center for Applied Research in Education books are available at quantity discounts with bulk purchase for educational, business, or sales promotional use. For information, please write to Prentice Hall Career & Personal Development Special Sales, 113 Sylvan Avenue, Englewood Cliffs, NJ 07632. Please supply: title of book, ISBN number, quantity, how the book will be used, date needed.

THE CENTER FOR APPLIED RESEARCH IN EDUCATION
West Nyack, NY 10994
A Simon & Schuster Company

On the World Wide Web at http://www.phdirect.com

Prentice Hall International (UK) Limited, *London*
Prentice Hall of Australia Pty. Limited, *Sydney*
Prentice Hall Canada, Inc., *Toronto*
Prentice Hall Hispanoamericana, S.A., *Mexico*
Prentice Hall of India Private Limited, *New Delhi*
Prentice Hall of Japan, Inc., *Tokyo*
Simon & Schuster Asia Pte. Ltd., *Singapore*
Editora Prentice Hall do Brasil, Ltda., *Rio de Janeiro*

DEDICATION

This volume is dedicated to
all of those children, young and grown
to adulthood, who have struggled to
overcome the effects of parental
drug and alcohol addiction.

ACKNOWLEDGMENTS

The authors wish to acknowledge Lieutenant James H. Pullan, Jr., Atlantic County, NJ Prosecutor's Office; Kathleen Hornberger, Parent-Child Educator, Family Center, Thomas Jefferson University; and Susan Kolwicz, our editor, for their assistance with this project.

ABOUT THE AUTHORS

Kathleen Pullan Watkins, Ed.D., received her education at Antioch and Temple Universities in Philadelphia, Pennsylvania. Her areas of specialization include early childhood education, parent-child attachment, and curriculum theory and program development. Dr. Watkins has had extensive experience as a teacher of young children, early childhood program director and consultant. She has served on the faculties at Temple University, Chestnut Hill College, and Penn State University, and presently serves as Assistant Professor of Early Childhood Education at Community College of Philadelphia. In recent years, Dr. Watkins worked as Parent-Child Specialist in a drug and alcohol treatment program, where she developed programs for pregnant and parenting women and their children. She is the co-author of six other books on early childhood, day care, and child development topics, including **Parent-Child Attachment: A Guide to Research**. Together with her partner of 23 years, Lucius Durant, she has written articles on special education that appeared in the **Target Management System**. She is the mother of a son (27) and a daughter (25).

Lucius Durant, Jr., M.Ed., received his education at Lincoln University (Pennsylvania) and Antioch University. In a career spanning nearly 40 years, he has held a wide range of positions in education and the human services. He has been a social worker, teacher of young children, and program director. Mr. Durant has worked extensively as a trainer of education staff, including teachers, principals and support staff, primarily for the School District of Philadelphia. He serves on the adjunct faculties of both Penn State University and Community College of Philadelphia, where he teaches courses in education, psychology, human development, and early childhood education. Mr. Durant has been a featured speaker at national conferences, and consults for local agencies and businesses. Together with Dr. Watkins, he is the author of **The Preschool Director's Staff Development Handbook** and **The Early Childhood Educator's Behavior Management Guide**. Mr. Durant's extensive family includes daughters ranging in age from 25 to 46 years. He has 15 grandchildren and 2 great-grandchildren.

FOREWORD

Substance Abuse has been one of the most profound social crises of the past two decades particularly in urban areas. Drug addiction is costly and devastating with social, political, and economic consequences. On a daily basis nearly every facet of our society is affected by substance abuse: families, schools, work arenas, health care, social service agencies, and the criminal justice system. In spite of the complex issues associated with substance abuse, the treatment field has continued to approach the problem from a disease perspective providing predominant medical services, frequently delivering those services to clients in isolation, and rarely interacting with diverse disciplines and professionals outside of the immediate treatment milieu. In addition, treatment providers have failed to educate external systems such as work arenas and social service agencies about the causes, management, and impact of substance abuse.

Consequently, nontreatment professionals who provide services directly and indirectly to substance abusers are often angry and frightened when faced with someone using drugs. Nurses and physicians are astonished that a pregnant addict continues to use drugs throughout her pregnancy. Social service providers are frustrated by the "late and missed appointment" syndrome of addicted individuals. Educators are concerned about children from substance-dependent families, but have no idea how to assist these families. Human resource managers are at a loss to deal with the impact of substance abuse on reduced workplace productivity and efficiency. And health care administrators are alarmed at rising costs due to undiagnosed addiction. Clearly, substance abuse is more than a medical issue—requiring a variety of approaches and solutions, across multiple settings.

Family Center of Thomas Jefferson University, a Philadelphia treatment program for pregnant substance abusers and their children has been at the forefront in the development of comprehensive and multidisciplinary models of treatment. Such models expand the notion of addiction—from a medical focus only to a multivariable phenomenon that is treated from a number of different perspectives including: biological/medical, psychological, social, economic, and political. This requires education advocacy, and mediation with schools, health care facilities, social service agencies, and workplaces in order to provide substance-dependent clients with necessary and supportive services.

In the late 1980s and early 1990s, Dr. Kathleen Watkins and I were part of the Family Center multidisciplinary team that consisted of OB/GYN physicians, a perinatal nurse specialist, social workers, psychiatrists, pharmacists, early childhood specialists, family planning experts, nutritionists, addictions counselors, researchers, and on occasion pro bono lawyers. Kathleen and I can speak to the difficulties of providing multidisciplinary treatment on both the micro and macro levels, in and out of the treatment milieu. For example, within our facility, each member of the team brought a methodical framework that would on occasion clash with the overall treatment plan for an individual client and the children of that client. Social workers and early childhood specialists struggled with balancing the clinical needs of the mothers with the developmental requirements of children. The early childhood specialists hoped to assess all children participating in the program in order to provide services where necessary and as soon as possible. This did not always occur, as mothers were frequently threatened by outside assessments and felt that they were being judged as parental failures. It took patience and serious clinical work to bring mothers to a point where they were able to allow their children full participation and evaluation in the children's programming. These kinds of problems forced staff to move beyond their disciplinary training, to become more flexible, and to alter various approaches to problems associated with addiction. The clinical social workers had to begin to include a child (or children) in the psychotherapeutic process of a mother; and the early childhood specialists had to respect the sometimes painful clinical course of a mother who needed time to meet the needs of her child(ren). Overall, these interactions provided a rich, productive, and synergistic experience for staff, clients, and their children.

Outside of the treatment facility, Kathleen, the staff, and I faced extraordinary prejudice against the clients we served due to a lack of understanding about the needs of the population. Pregnant women were denied access to inpatient detoxification units because of physician/hospital fear of legal recourse around the complications of drug addiction and pregnancy, yet our program was expected to detoxify these same pregnant women on an outpatient basis. Homeless women and children were refused shelter because the mothers were prescribed methadone by our physicians for opiate withdrawal, or psychotropic medications for depression. Staff members in the shelters were "philosophically opposed to any kind of prescription drug therapy for addicted individuals." These shelters would not consider, however, denying access to someone on medication for diabetes or high blood pressure. A number of recovering women were expelled from GED, literacy, and job training programs when they disclosed past drug addiction, or because of methadone maintenance. And furthermore, in spite of our program's advocacy, Child Protective Services removed several children from mothers who were in the program and sober—and at times, that very same organization failed to place children assessed by our specialists to be in imminent danger due to parental drug use. Each of these examples points to the profound need to educate and support the systems and individuals who come into contact with and provide services to substance abusers and their families.

This book is a systematic attempt to assist those professionals in understanding and managing the complex issues associated with drug dependence.

Kathleen Watkins and Lucius Durant have integrated their vast experience treating the children of substance abusers with a corresponding depth and feeling for the chemically dependent parent. The book provides a comprehensive and balanced view of the problems of addiction and the impact on various systems, and presents precise and summary methods that are meant to assist professionals in the provision of effective services to substance abusers and their children.

Working with Children and Families Affected by Substance Abuse is a valuable and rare resource for a variety of professionals who have contact with substance-dependent individuals. The practical overview and the hands-on guidelines allow professionals in need of specific information to pick and choose data that are useful and relevant for diverse situations and settings. It should be a required text in academia across disciplines, and a necessary addition to the libraries of social service agencies and other relevant work settings.

T. Hagan, Ph.D.
Treatment Research Institute
Philadelphia, PA

INTRODUCTION

As we prepare to enter the 21st century, the abusive use of drugs and alcohol continues largely unabated. As the epidemic has worsened, the statistics are staggering. Among the industrialized nations of the world, the United States leads in the rates of substance abuse: (1) One-fourth of America's children admit to use of one or more illicit drugs. (2) By some estimates, three-quarters of a million drug-exposed babies are born annually in the United States. Substance abuse is at the root of a myriad of family and social problems. Among these are homelessness, unemployment, inadequate education, nutrition and other health problems, unprotected sexual activity with resulting pregnancy and sexually transmitted disease, and dysfunctional family relationships. (3) In spite of the best efforts of law enforcement, health care and human service professionals, barely a dent has been made in efforts to quell the use of drugs. Furthermore, it has become increasingly apparent that no community is free from the impact of substance abuse, as families from every cultural, social, and economic spectrum have been affected.

Media coverage and reporting of the drug epidemic has been confusing and overwhelming. While alerting us to the problem, the media have also painted an ugly portrait of drug suppliers, users, and their children. Many of those working in direct service to families have been at a loss as to how to respond. Unless our training is in addictions counseling, we have had few resources for confronting drug abuse or its related consequences. We have often felt powerless in the face of what seems like an insurmountable social crisis.

Working with Children and Families Affected by Substance Abuse is written for early childhood educators and others who work with children and families. It is designed to provide some clarity and to offer guidelines for those who want to attempt intervention with substance-affected families. It is not a definitive work on the subject. It will not make anyone an expert on the addictions problem. We leave that to researchers and others with expertise in the field of treatment. Instead, it is intended to be a resource, used in concert with consultations and additional readings. Wherever possible, we have included both endnotes and resources to give readers further sources of information.

We have attempted to address key topics of interest to educators and human service providers, with a focus on the impact of substance exposure on children and their environments.

In Chapter One the scope of the drug and alcohol problem in the United States is addressed. Drugs in current use are described, along with their street names and effects. The characteristics of substance-abusing women and men are discussed. While abuse occurs among all groups of people, research has highlighted some significant features of the history and lifestyle of many of those who become addicted. Some of the variations in treatment models are also discussed.

The impact of substance abuse on the family is explored in Chapter Two, including the dynamics of family interaction. Problems of domestic violence, child abuse, and neglect in relation to parental addiction are described. Issues of health, such as AIDS and tuberculosis, as well as homelessness, are discussed as they affect those with addictions and their children.

The focus of Chapter Three is parenting skills. Substance abuse is known to adversely affect parental competence, and to impact on rates of child abuse and neglect. This chapter looks also at the growth of skills as parents experience the recovery process, and roles for human service workers are explored.

Chapter Four is devoted to clarifying the impact of prenatal and environmental substance exposure* on children. It explodes some of the many myths surrounding the effects of crack and other drugs on the unborn, while looking at the harsher realities of prenatal exposure to alcohol.

Having identified problems of the drug-exposed newborn in the previous chapter, in Chapter Five we offer suggestions for those working with infants and young toddlers. Holding, comforting, and feeding techniques are described. The controversy surrounding breastfeeding and addiction is discussed, as well as other issues for addictive parents.

Chapter Six focuses on programming for substance-exposed toddlers, preschoolers, and primary school children. Methods are suggested for planning the environment and for daily scheduling. The importance of selecting appropriate staff is emphasized.

In Chapter Seven we offer a series of activities to promote parent education, child development, and parent and child experiences. These activities are designed to develop self-awareness, language, and social concepts, among other skills.

In Chapter Eight we have addressed advocacy roles for those working with substance-affected families. The need for networking among those in health, education, social work, and legal professions is stressed.

We have also included a bibliography and Appendix featuring resources for those interested in further reading, or tools for drug and alcohol education, and a list of relevant agencies.

The key message of *Working with Children and Families Affected by Substance Abuse* is one of hope. We believe that substance abusers and their children should be supported and assisted in order to recover and become fully functioning members of the human family.

---

* In this volume "environmental substance exposure" refers to children living in environments where others abuse drugs.

After many years of work in the human services field, we still believe that one caring and knowledgeable individual can make a difference in the life of a parent and child. We hope that this book can be a tool for making that difference.

Kathleen Pullan Watkins, Ed.D. and Lucius Durant, Jr., M.Ed.

ENDNOTES

1. Newcomb, M.D., and Bentler, P.M. "Substance Use and Abuse Among Children and Teenagers," *American Psychologist.* 44, 1989, pp. 242–8.

2. *National Household Survey on Drug Abuse: 1988*: Rockville, MD: National Institute on Drug Abuse, U.S. Department of Health and Human Services.

3. Gans, J.E. *America's Adolescents: How Healthy Are They?* Vol.1. Chicago: American Medical Association, 1991.

What Do You Know About the Substance Abuse Problem?

Directions: Before reading this book take a few minutes to ask yourself what you know about the substance abuse problem. Answer "yes" or "no" to each of the ten questions below. You will find the same quiz and an answer key on page 159 of this volume.

1. Drugs are primarily an urban problem. _____

2. Men abuse drugs substantially more often than women. _____

3. Drug addicts can generally recover after two to three months in a treatment program. _____

4. Drug and alcohol treatment is usually available in prison for people who request it. _____

5. If women are HIV positive and pregnant, their babies will generally develop AIDS. _____

6. Children who are prenatally exposed to cocaine often have physical deformities and/or mental deficits. _____

7. Marijuana is safe for use by pregnant women. _____

8. The most widely used drug is cocaine. _____

9. Drug use is generally triggered by teenage experimentation with cigarettes and alcohol. _____

10. Parents who abuse drugs usually abuse their children. _____

CONTENTS

CHAPTER THREE
Drug Abuse and Parenting   35

CHAPTER FOUR
Drugs, Alcohol, and Children   51

CHAPTER FIVE
Caring for Prenatally Drug-Exposed Children   69

CHAPTER SIX
Developing Programs for
Substance-Affected Children   89

CHAPTER SEVEN
Activities for Parent Education and Child Development   105

CHAPTER EIGHT
Networking and Advocating with Human Service Delivery Systems   141

CHAPTER ONE

The Substance-Abuse Problem

According to the 1992 National Household Survey on Drug Abuse, more than 74 million Americans have used drugs (1). In the last quarter century, substance abuse has been recognized as one of our most serious problems, affecting every social, economic, and cultural group in the United States. Even occasional drug or alcohol use is potentially harmful, but it is the abuse of substances that is the most devastating. The U.S. Department of Justice defines addiction as "the compulsive use of a drug resulting in physical, psychological, or social harm to the user and the continued use despite that harm (2)." Substance abuse can lead to psychological addiction, to physical dependence, or to both of these. In any case, use of the drug becomes essential to functioning and to a sense of well-being.

Drug and alcohol addiction has severe effects for most users. Addiction interferes with daily living, relationships, and the health of the user. In the effort to obtain drugs, education, employment, and family life may become irrelevant. The user may risk health and personal safety. Injuries, often from gunshot wounds may occur while attempting to secure illicit substances, and street drugs are not necessarily pure in content; they may be mixed with other toxic material that can cause adverse reactions, even death. Medical complications can occur suddenly in a novice or in an experienced user. Some of the potential negative reactions include the interruption of normal heart rhythm, rapid elevation of blood pressure, respiratory failure, even psychiatric problems. Researchers have found that repeated use of certain drugs, such as heroin, can compromise an individual's immune system, creating heightened susceptibility to many kinds of infection. Many long-term drug users develop chronic health problems and disease. Hepatitis and HIV exposure can result from intravenous drug use. According to the Drug Abuse Warning Network, in 1990 nearly 6,000 people in 27 cities died from drug-related causes (3).

The National Household Survey of 1992, which studied a representative group of more than 69,000 Americans, found that 67 percent of respondents used either alcohol or an illicit drug. Alcohol, the most widely used substance by both children and adults, is consumed by an estimated 170 million people. Marijuana use comes in a distant second with more than 67 million users, while 23 million Americans use some form of cocaine. There is nonmedical use of prescription drugs by an estimated 24 million persons, and 146 million Americans smoke cigarettes.

The National Institute on Drug Abuse regularly surveys a range of special populations, including high school seniors, American military personnel, and incarcerated persons, about their drug and alcohol use. Nearly half of the secondary school students (4) and 80 percent of prison inmates (5) admitted to substance use. Although some studies suggest that drug use begins around age 21, other research indicates that it may start as early as 12 (6) or 15 (7) years.

A disturbing report was recently issued by the Parents' Resource Institute for Drug Education. In a 1994–1995 survey of 200,000 junior and senior high school students in 32 states, a rise in teen use of drugs was cited for the fourth year in a row. Among those surveyed, 28.1 percent of children in grades six through eight have smoked cigarettes, 9.5 percent have used marijuana, and 30.8 percent have tried beer (8).

In the past, drug and alcohol abuse were considered urban problems, associated with city life and poverty. However, the National Survey suggests that substance abuse is not more prevalent in cities. In fact, the rate of alcohol use is slightly higher in rural areas.

While there is extensive information available on some population groups, little is known about others. For example, data on substance abuse among school truants, dropouts and the homeless is sparse. In any event, the National Institute on Drug Abuse indicates that all estimates of drug use are probably low, due to the difficult-to-reach populations and to the self-reporting nature of surveys.

Factors Influencing Drug Use

Addiction to drugs and alcohol is found in every class and group of people in the United States. While there are few specific characteristics of drug users, there do appear to be factors that are associated with the onset of use and with addiction.

Among adolescents, drug use may begin with early use of tobacco or alcohol. Children may be more susceptible to addiction if drugs or alcohol have been abused in the home by parents or siblings. Involvement with peers who experiment with drugs can be a factor, along with a teen's participation in delinquent activities. These adolescents may also have strong feelings of social alienation and more than the usual tendencies toward rebelliousness. Low self-esteem and an orientation toward risk-taking behavior also seem to play a role. It is unclear whether the poor school performance of adolescents who use drugs and alcohol is a cause or an effect of the problem.

Among substance abusers there are many families in which there is inconsistent parenting and a lack of closeness and communication; the result is often family conflict and even violence. Parents of addicts also tend to be poor disciplinarians, therefore, children lack guidelines for appropriate behavior. Addicted parents often have difficulty setting boundaries in their relationships with their children. Overinvolvement (see Chapter Three) is a common problem for some, while others are unable to form close emotional bonds. Levels of education and rates of employment are lower among using than nonusing individuals; consequently, they can recall fewer success experiences. Some addicted persons suffer from depression and other psychiatric disorders. Their drug use may be a way of relieving anxiety and achieving an acceptable level of social interaction. Among drug dependent women, one researcher documented high levels of physical and sexual assault, including incest (9). These incidences may not only contribute to drug use, but prohibit the woman from having many types of normal, adult-level relationships (see Figure 1.1).

According to the National Household Survey, males are more likely to use drugs and alcohol than females, and those in the 18-to-25 age range are more apt to be involved in current substance abuse. Heroin is the drug of choice among more women than men (57.3 percent compared to 42.7 percent). Cocaine, however, is used by 70.1 percent men versus 29.9 percent women. Both African-Americans and whites are more likely to abuse drugs than Hispanics (10).

Figure 1.1
Factors Influencing Drug/Alcohol Use in Children and Adults

Personal Traits / Behaviors

- low self-esteem
- orientation toward risk-taking behavior
- early alcohol, tobacco use
- feelings of alienation, rebelliousness
- depression, mental health problems

Family Factors

- parental substance-abuse problems
- poor familial communication, lack of closeness or over-involvement
- inconsistent parenting
- lack of discipline
- child abuse/neglect
- experience with significant, early loss of a primary caretaker

Other Influences

- peer pressure
- poor school performance
- delinquent behavior
- low level of education
- poor employment history

Trends in Drug and Alcohol Use

Government studies have been indicating that drug use probably peaked between 1977 and 1982; however, some new research shows findings that conflict with government reports (11). Cocaine abuse, for example, has not decreased significantly for any gender, age, or racial group (12). The Drug Abuse Warning Network had also reported a decrease in drug-related medical emergencies since the late 1980s, but is now indicating a rise in cocaine-related hospital admissions (13). In spite of tremendous efforts on the part of law enforcement agencies, parents, and schools, there are still millions of Americans abusing drugs and alcohol, and the acquisition and production of illicit substances bring billions of dollars to individuals and foreign markets. This is not the time to rest, but a time to arm ourselves and to continue to do battle. Educating both children and adults about the serious nature of this problem is one way to combat the substance-abuse dilemma.

Key Drugs of Abuse and Their Effects

In Figure 1.2 we have provided readers with a chart showing commonly used drugs and their immediate or acute effects on the user. These drugs have been divided into the following types: alcohol, cocaine, opiates, marijuana, depressants, stimulants, hallucinogens, inhalants, and anabolic steroids. Some of these can be legally obtained. Even those that are available by prescription can be abused. Each of these has the potential to create physical or psychological dependence. Some are consumed in liquid form, while others are sniffed, or smoked, or injected, or swallowed in capsule form. Some users take prescription drugs, open several different types of capsules, mix the contents together, and repackage them in an empty capsule. The initial impact of the substances shown on the chart can last for as little as one hour and for as long as 24 hours. Some drugs, in particular the hallucinogens, have the ability to create flashback effects days or weeks after the drug was first used. All of these substances are widely available. It is said that there are few places in the United States to which one could travel and not be able to acquire his or her drug of choice; drugs have invaded the community, the home, and the workplace.

Figure 1.2
Key Substances of Abuse and Their Effects

Type of Drug	Street Name(s)	Methods of Use	Short-Term Effects *	Duration of Acute Effects
Alcohol		consumed in alcoholic beverages	euphoria, drowsiness, dizziness, slurred speech, staggering, stupor	1 hr/drink
Cocaine/ Crack	C, coke, snow, nose candy, rock, french fries, girl	sniffed (cocaine) smoked, injected (crack)	euphoria, energy, rapid heartbeat/ breathing, high body temperature, dilated pupils, sweating, pallor	1–2 hours
Opiates (heroin, opium, Demerol, morphine)	H, horse, junk, smack, boy, dope, DO	injected or sniffed	pleasure, stupor, vomiting, increased urination, constipation, sweating, itchy skin, slowed breathing	3–6 hours
Marijuana/ Hashish	pot, grass, weed, reefer, Columbian, blunts, hash	smoked or cooked with food/eaten	relaxation, reduced inhibition, impaired coordination/balance, rapid heartbeat, red eyes, dry mouth/throat, impaired motor skills/ concentration/short-term memory	2–4 hours
Depressants (sleeping pills, tranquilizers, sedating antihistamines)	bennies, reds, red birds, red devils, red hearts, downers, blue heavens, purple hearts	swallowed in tablet or capsule form	slowed central nervous system activity, relaxation, sense of well-being, slurred speech, staggering, blurred vision, impaired thinking/perception, slowed reflexes/breathing	1–24 hours

*Not to be used to diagnose addiction or drug use. Symptoms may be those of other disease or sickness.

Figure 1.2 (continued)
Key Substances of Abuse and Their Effects

Type of Drug	*Street Name(s)*	*Methods of Use*	*Short-Term Effects* *	*Duration of Acute Effects*
Stimulants (amphetamines, methamphetimines)	uppers, speed, meth, crank, dexies, crystal, ice, white crosses, crystal meth, chalk, glass, go, zip, chris, chrisy	swallowed in tablet or capsule form	increased alertness, rapid heartbeat/ breathing, dilated pupils, dry mouth, aggressive/ bizarre behavior, hallucinations, tremors, severe paranoia	2–4 hours
Hallucinogens (LSD and PCP)	acid, dust, angel dust	taken orally as drops, powder, pellets	dilated pupils, nausea, dizziness, muscle weakness/ stiffness, rapid reflexes, increased body temperature/ blood pressure, loss of appetite, altered perceptions, impaired thought processes/short term memory, extreme mood swings	2–12 hours with potential for flash-backs
Inhalants (solvents, aerosol nitrates)	sniffing, huffing	inhaled from bag or saturated cloth, inhaled directly from can, or by spraying into a small bag	lightheadedness, slowed breathing/ heartbeat/ other functions, slurred speech, ringing in ears	Variable
Anabolic steroids		orally or injected	feeling of well-being, increased energy, heightened blood pressure, tissue growth, rapid weight gain, water/oil retention, aggressive behavior, increased male sex characteristics	N/A

*Not to be used to diagnose addiction or drug use.

The Social and Economic Costs of Drug Abuse

As disastrous as the effects of abuse are for the drug user, they are equally hazardous to the rest of society. Virtually no one in the United States is untouched by the substance-abuse problem. While there are obvious financial, health and economic consequences, there are also costs to the overall well-being and mental health of the population in general.

Many of the increases in violence in our society can be traced to drug trafficking and use. Robberies, assaults, and homicides are linked directly to the substance-abuse problem. As a result, the costs of insuring one's health, automobiles, and homes have increased. Perhaps even more disastrous are the psychological effects. People feel unsafe in their own homes and neighborhood, afraid of becoming the victims of drug users and pushers.

Similar impacts have been felt in the schools. Some children are truant because school buildings are no longer safe places. Learning is interfered with and educational costs have been increased by the addition of counselors, security personnel, and metal detectors.

Health care costs have been dramatically increased by drug and alcohol use. Drug-related problems account for a high percentage of emergency room visits and hospitalizations. Insurance companies must now include drug and alcohol treatment in their coverage. Many instances of child abuse and neglect, including those needing medical intervention, are related to parental or caregiver substance abuse.

The workplace, too, has been affected by drug and alcohol problems. Loss of productivity resulting from employee addiction is but one effect. Some workers are absent from work because family members or friends have drug-related problems. Some work-related accidents are associated with substance abuse. In addition, many companies have been forced to include drug testing, counseling and treatment as features of employee services. Products may be inferior or defective as a result of drug use, and those persons who serve the public directly and also use drugs may endanger others.

Entire neighborhoods have been changed by drug use. Property values have declined and property damage has resulted when drug dealers move into communities. People are forced to live barricaded in their homes and often feel powerless to combat the violence around them.

Law enforcement has felt the impact vis-à-vis the need to create special narcotics departments and task forces. In recent years, drug and alcohol abuse has also cost the lives of many officers. Many in criminal justice will admit there are simply not enough police nor enough money to adequately deal with the problem. The courts are clogged with drug-related cases, and the prisons filled with perpetrators of drug-related crimes.

Not the least of the social costs of drug and alcohol abuse is its impact on families. There is an untold degree of pain and suffering experienced by those victimized by the drug problem. Some of those affected are the relatives of addicts, the survivors of victims of drive-by shootings, and the relatives of drug-exposed infants and children.

The federal government and other agencies estimate that as many as three-quarters of a million drug-affected babies may be born annually in the United States (14). The social impacts can include long-term hospitalization of the infant, special education, and social services intervention for the child and family. Furthermore, drug-exposed children are more likely to experience subsequent hospitalizations.

In part because the full extent of substance abuse is unknown, the full range of social and economic costs of substance abuse can never be accurately measured; we can only estimate the toll taken on individuals, families and institutions.

Substance-Abuse Treatment

Drug- and alcohol-abuse treatment may be publicly or privately administered; may be profit or nonprofit making; and can be funded by foundations, government agencies, fees charged to patients, or insurance companies. The National Drug and Alcohol Treatment Unit Survey defines a drug treatment facility as one having a structured and formal mechanism for treatment and/or recovery, including services and a budget allocated for this purpose (15). The Survey also indicates that 1,000,000 people are treated annually for addiction. Three to four times this number, however, are in need of treatment services, and there are insufficient numbers of programs to meet their needs. Most people do not enter treatment programs willingly. They do so under pressure from family, friends, health professionals, or the criminal justice system.

THE SETTINGS

There are two primary types of treatment facilities. The nonresidential or outpatient variety provides services at a particular site; however, the client lives elsewhere. Programs of this type often serve special populations, such as women, the elderly, or cocaine abusers. They may serve from 100 up to 1,000 clients at any given time. More than half of the drug treatment programs in the country are outpatient (see Figure 1.3).

The second major type of program is the residential or inpatient facility. This setting might be a hospital, or a group or halfway house. The client lives at the site and receives a range of services, such as psychotherapy or counseling, job skills training, and parenting skills training. Up to 50 clients live in residential settings. Approximately 20 percent of treatment is residential; the remaining 26 percent of treatment services are of the mixed service type.

TREATMENT MODALITIES

The term *treatment modality* refers to the chief manner in which treatment is provided. In this category, there are a range of treatment methods available (16). Some programs provide a combination of these in an effort to address the client's needs.

Detoxification involves planning and implementing the client's program of gradual withdrawal from drugs. This tends to be a highly individualized process in which relapse can and often does occur. This form of treatment sometimes includes medication designed to alleviate the problems associated with withdrawal.

Pharmacologic assistance is provided in response to some kinds of addiction. Medications are used to counter the effects of the addictive drugs. Methadone maintenance of heroin-addicted persons is a prime example of this form of treatment. The use of methadone, first authorized in 1974 under the Narcotic Addiction Treatment Act, is controversial in addiction treatment. In the best possible of circumstances, the heroin addict receives counseling and a steadily declining dose of methadone until he or she is eventually drug free. In individual situations , however, some persons in recovery may receive doses of methadone over many years. Some argue that this type of treatment substitutes one addiction for another, yet when properly supervised and administered methadone does not interfere with an individual's daily functioning.

Also controversial is the use of methadone to aid in the treatment and recovery of pregnant women. Opponents cite the instance of neonatal abstinence syndrome among infants prenatally exposed to methadone—a newborn, prenatally exposed to drugs, undergoes withdrawal in the days after birth. Methadone advocates note the increase in prenatal care, maternal nutrition, and full-term births when women are in supervised treatment programs.

Therapeutic interventions are found in most treatment programs. These can vary greatly due to the program setting, staff expertise, and services provided; however, they generally include counseling and behavioral therapy. This may occur as group or individual intervention.

Self-help and 12-step support groups are some of the original treatment modalities for addiction—they bring together persons with similar problems for peer support and counseling. The purpose is both achieving freedom from addiction and remaining drug free. Many support groups, including Cocaine Anonymous and Narcotics Anonymous, are modeled after the Alcoholics Anonymous 12-step program. Advantages of these programs include their accessibility in most communities, and the fact that they are usually free to anyone who needs the service. Support groups also provide 24-hour peer support as an aid in relapse prevention.

A form of treatment involving both a special setting and unique modalities is the therapeutic community. This is a residential treatment facility in which admission to the program and rules are often determined by the clients themselves with treatment staff as facilitators. During the time spent in this setting, the individual also works on developing social, family, educational and occupational skills necessary for survival and continued sobriety. Many residential programs specify that clients remain drug and alcohol free for the duration of their treatment.

In case management, a social worker or addictions counselor is involved with a client on a one-to-one basis. By developing an ongoing relationship with the person in treatment, the counselor hopes to explore the causes and triggers of substance abuse. The case manager may also help the client to address other basic needs, such as those for housing, child care, or health care.

THE EFFECTIVENESS OF DRUG TREATMENT

There are few studies demonstrating high levels of success resulting from specific drug therapies. A number of issues must be considered in evaluating treatment success. For example, drug abuse is a chronic problem, often involving relapse and improvement occurring in small increments. Full recovery may take many years and experience with a number of types of intervention. A client might require a period of residential treatment, followed by an outpatient program, combined with years of peer support. In fact, recovery based on any one period of treatment is rare.

Even persons suffering from the same types of addiction can be influenced by very different life situations and complicating factors. Therefore, all treatment programs cannot help all clients. A person may have to participate in several before finding the program that is most beneficial to him or her.

Figure 1.3
Settings and Modalities for Substance-abuse Treatment

Nonresidential / Outpatient Settings

- services provided on site
- client lives elsewhere
- serves large numbers of clients

Residential / Inpatient Services

- broad range of services may be provided
- client lives in-house
- up to 50 clients served

Treatment Modalities

- detoxification—planned gradual withdrawal from drugs/alcohol
- pharmacologic assistance—medications used to neutralize drug's effects
- therapeutic intervention—counseling and/or behavioral therapy
- support group—peer support/counseling meetings modeled after AA
- therapeutic community—residential setting run by clients with strict rules and programs to help client with full functioning in outside world
- case management—one-to-one counseling and support to address addiction and overall life needs

Finally, it is unwise to use only decreased drug use as a measure of treatment success. Long before full recovery is achieved, many individuals have increased self-esteem and improved health and lifestyle, and they have become more effective parents.

Drug Abuse Prevention Efforts

Many individuals and groups across the country have become involved in efforts to reduce the instance of substance abuse. Among these are churches, schools, community groups, and law enforcement agencies. Materials have been developed and books written aimed at age groups from the preschool years through adulthood (see Appendixes). The media have contributed via special programming and public service announcements.

There are two forms of prevention: Primary focuses on stopping the onset of abuse, and secondary is aimed at preventing continued use by those who are minimally involved (17). Both of these efforts have similar objectives. First, they attempt to educate people about the adverse effects of and problems associated with drug use. Second, they provide techniques for resisting pressure to use drugs. Third, they motivate community involvement in drug use prevention activities, such as offering alternative events for teenagers.

It is not known whether drug and alcohol education has played a role in the recent decline in substance abuse. It is certain, however, that prevention efforts must continue. The only way to end the drug- and alcohol-abuse epidemic is to reduce the demand for drugs, and to put the drug traffickers and dealers out of business forever.

Endnotes

1. *National Household Survey on Drug Abuse: Main Findings*. Washington, DC: United States Department of Health and Human Services, 1992.

2. *Annual Medical Examiner Data 1990, Data from the Drug Abuse Warning Network. Series 1*, Number 10-B, 1991.

3. Bureau of Justice Statistics. *A National Report: Drugs, Crime, and the Justice System*. Washington, DC: United States Department of Justice, December 1992.

4. Johnston, L.D., P.M. O'Malley, and J.G. Bachman. *Drug Use Among American High School Seniors, College Students, and Young Adults, 1975–1990*. Volumes 1 and 2. Washington, DC: United States Department of Health and Human Services, 1991.

5. Bureau of Justice Statistics. *Profile of State Prison Inmates, 1986, Special Report*. Washington, DC: United States Department of Justice, 1988.

6. Hagan,T.A., "A Retrospective Search for the Etiology of Drug Abuse: A Background Comparison of a Drug-addicted Population of Women and a Group of Nonaddicted Women," In National Institute on Drug Abuse Monograph Series, *Problems of Drug Dependence*, No. 81. Washington, DC: United States Department of Health and Human Services, 1987.

7. Bureau of Justice Statistics. *Profile of State Prison Inmates, 1986, Special Report*. Washington, DC: United States Department of Justice, 1988.

8. Weiner, J., "Getting Hooked," *Philadelphia Inquirer*, November 12, 1995, pp. H1 and H6.

9. Hagan, T.A., "A Retrospective Search for the Etiology of Drug Abuse: A Background Comparison of a Drug-addicted Population of Women and a Group of Nonaddicted Women," In National Institute on Drug Abuse Monograph Series, *Problems of Drug Dependence*, No. 81. Washington, DC: United States Department of Health and Human Services, 1987.

10. *National Household Survey on Drug Abuse: Main Findings*. Washington, DC: United States Department of Human Services, 1992.

11. Harrison, J., "Trends in Illicit Drug Use in the United States: Conflicting Results from National Surveys." *International Journal of the Addictions*, Vol. 27, 1992, pp. 817–847.

12. *National Household Survey on Drug Abuse: Main Findings*. Washington, DC: United States Department of Human Services, 1992.

13. *Annual Medical Examiner Data 1990, Data from the Drug Abuse Warning Network*, Series 1, Number 10-B, 1991.

14. Gomby, D.S., and P.H. Shiono. "Estimating the Number of Substance-exposed Infants," In *The Future of Children*, 1(1) 1991, pp. 17–25.

15. ADAMHA, *National Drug and Alcoholism Treatment Unit Survey* (NDATUS), 1989 Main Findings Report, 1990.

16. Saxe, L., and G. Schusterman, "Drug Treatment Modalities: Taxonomy to Aid Development of Services Research," In *Drug Abuse Services Research Series: Background Papers on Drug Abuse Financing and Services Research*. Washington, DC: National Institute on Drug Abuse, 1991, pp. 1–5.

17. Bureau of Justice Statistics. *A National Report: Drugs, Crime, and the Justice System*. Washington, DC: United States Department of Justice, December 1992.

Resources

Backer, T.E. *Evaluations of the 1991 National Conference on Drug Abuse Research and Practice*. Report prepared for National Institute on Drug Abuse. Washington, DC: NIDA, 1991.

Ball, J.C., and A. Ross. *The Effectiveness of Methadone Maintenance Treatment*. New York: Springer-Verlag, 1991.

Chatlos, C. Crack: *What You Should Know About the Cocaine Epidemic*. New York: Perigree Books, 1987.

Cocaine Treatment: Research and Clinical Perspectives. Washington, DC: United States Department of Health and Human Services, 1993.

Coombs, R.H. (Ed.). *The Family Context of Adolescent Drug Use*. Binghamton, NY: Haworth Press, 1988.

De La Rosa, M., et al (Eds.). *Drugs and Violence: Causes, Correlates and Consequences*. NIDA Research Monograph, No. 103. Washington, DC: United States Department of Health and Human Services, 1991.

Doshan, T., and C. Bursch. "Women and Substance Abuse: Critical Issues in Treatment Design." *Journal of Drug Education*. 12 (3), 1982.

Gans, J.E. *America's Adolescents: How Healthy Are They?* Vol. 1. Chicago, IL: American Medical Association, 1991.

Inhalant Abuse: A Volatile Research Agenda. NIDA Research Monograph No. 129. United States Department of Health and Human Services, 1992.

Institute on Medicine. *Broadening the Base of Treatment for Alcohol Problems*. Washington, DC: National Academy Press, 1990.

Institute on Medicine. *Causes and Consequences of Alcohol Problems*. Washington, DC: National Academy Press, 1987.

Institute on Medicine. *Treating Drug Problems*, Vol. 1. Washington, DC: National Academy Press, 1990.

Johnston, L.D., J.G. Bachman, and P.M. O'Malley. *Drug Use, Drinking and Smoking: National Survey Results from High School, College, and Young Adult Populations*. Rockville, MD: National Institute on Drug Abuse, 1991.

Leukefeld, C.G., and F.M. Tims (Eds.). *Drug Abuse Treatment in Prisons and Jails*. NIDA Research Monograph No. 118. Washington, DC: United States Department of Health and Human Services, 1992.

Lin, G.C. and L. Erinoff (Eds.). *Anabolic Steroid Use*. NIDA Research Monograph No. 102. Washington, DC: United States Department of Health and Human Services, 1991.

National Association for Perinatal Addiction Research and Education. *National Hospital Incidence Survey (NAPARE Update)*. Chicago, IL: NAPARE, September 1988.

Onken, L.S., J.D. Blaine and J.J. Borem (Eds.). *Behavioral Treatments for Drug Abuse and Dependence*. NIDA Research Monograph No. 137. Washington, DC: United States Department of Health and Human Services, 1993.

Pickens, R.W., C.G. Leukefeld and C.R. Schuster. *Improving Drug Use Treatment*. NIDA Research Monograph No. 106. Washington, DC: United States Department of Health and Human Services, 1992.

Schinke, S.P., G.J. Botvin and M.A. Orlandi. *Substance Abuse in Children and Adolescents*. Newbury Park, CA: Sage, 1991.

Segal, B. (ed.). *Perspectives in Adolescent Drug Use*. Binghamton, New York: Haworth Press, 1989.

Steinberg, L. *Adolescent Transitions and Substance Abuse Prevention*. Monograph commissioned and distributed by the Office for Substance Abuse Prevention. Washington, DC: The Office, 1989.

The State of America's Children: 1995. Washington, DC: Children's Defense Fund, 1995.

CHAPTER TWO

Substance-Abuse: Impact on the Family

Addicts and alcoholics are not the only victims of substance abuse. Parents and grandparents, spouses and children are all affected. The exact relationship of social problems to drug and alcohol abuse is not known. It is unclear whether substance abuse is the cause of difficulties, or whether addiction results from social and emotional problems. In this chapter we will explore some of the social dilemmas often associated with substance abuse. We will attempt to understand how various problems spiral out to engulf the family and the community.

Domestic Violence

Physical or emotional assault on a spouse has a well-documented relationship to addictions. Domestic violence is a problem in the relationship between two people that centers around the perpetrator's need to control the victim. While spousal abuse has existed as long as there has been intimacy between adults, it has come to the forefront of national attention only in the past few years. With cases of celebrity spousal battering and homicide, the doors have finally been thrown open to reveal the tip of a serious social problem.

In the past, reports of domestic violence were, if not ignored altogether, treated as private, family matters. Even when a woman seemed to be in fear for her life, unless she agreed to press charges against her abuser, there would seldom be an arrest of her assailant. At present, only half of the 50 states mandate an arrest if domestic abuse is determined to have been violent. In spite of some continuing apathy about spousal abuse, there have been some responses to the problem. Community and women's groups have organized to provide crisis counseling and shelters. Recent media campaigns have urged those who suspect victimization of a friend or relative to report the problem to authorities (see Figure 2.1).

Meanwhile, the domestic violence statistics are staggering. An estimated two million people are battered by spouses or partners every year in the United States. There are 30,000 emergency room visits and 100,000 days annually of hospitalization that result from spousal abuse. As many as 2,500 women are killed each year by an abusive partner (1).

As with many other social problems, the exact causes of domestic violence are unknown; however, researchers are beginning to identify some of the factors prevalent in spousal abuse. Some abusers are known to have witnessed violence as children. They may have been prevented from learning healthy ways of expressing anger, disappointment, even love. Women who are exposed to violence in childhood are at greater risk for victimization in adult life. They may have a tendency to choose mates who abuse them in the same ways that their mothers were abused. They may even believe that battering is one way that love is expressed. A teenage girl appearing on a television talk show said of her abusing boyfriend, "He only beats girls that he loves."

Personality factors (such as aggressive tendencies) or mental health disorders may also play a role in the instance of domestic violence. Researchers found that a high percentage of battering men suffer from depression-related disorders. In some cases, treatment with antidepressive medications lessened the frequency of aggressive and violent behaviors.

The use of drugs and alcohol has also been linked to spousal abuse. Many of those who experience domestic violence report that their abuser had been drinking prior to battering incidents. In cases of severe assaults against partners, one study showed, alcohol had been used by 70 percent of the abusers (2).

While there are few statistics to indicate the role played by drug abuse in domestic violence, one researcher has speculated about this relationship (3). He suggests that some drug use leads to excitable, even irrational, behavior that can lead to spousal abuse. It is noted, however, that the effects of some drugs include drowsiness and stupor. These may actually counter the violent tendencies of some abusers.

A second scenario for domestic violence occurs when an addict steals money or goods from family members in order to buy drugs. A confrontation of the substance abuser may lead to spousal abuse. The third situation is one in which an angry or fearful spouse reports drug use to the authorities, and is battered for the perceived betrayal.

Some abusing partners may intentionally drink alcohol or abuse drugs prior to violent incidents. Substance abuse may be a way of rationalizing the abusive behavior that would not otherwise be tolerated. In other words, "You know I didn't mean it! I had too much to drink!"

Substance abuse plays yet another role in domestic violence. Studies indicate that women who abuse drugs and alcohol may themselves be at greater risk for domestic violence. Not only are these women more frequently battered, but the abuse is more likely to be severe. There are several reasons for this vulnerability. Women who drink alcohol and use drugs are viewed as lowest on the social scale, even by other addicts and alcoholics. Aggressive, loud behavior by a female substance abuser is more likely to be seen as embarrassing and socially unacceptable. Finally, women who use drugs and alcohol are often involved in relationships with partners who are addicts—a volatile and dangerous mix.

The interrelationship of domestic violence to substance abuse is one that is in need of further study. If, as research suggests, violence in childhood predisposes a person to substance abuse and possibly to spousal abuse in adult life, additional studies may lead to strategies for breaking the cycles of individual and family destruction.

Figure 2.1
Signs and Symptoms of Domestic Violence

- Frequent, unexplained bruises, cuts, or other injuries
- Frequent emergency room visits
- Social isolation of abused partner or entire family
- A controlling or extremely jealous partner
- Drug and/or alcohol abuse by one or both partners
- Poor impulse control on the part of the abusing partner
- Low self-esteem of one or both partners
- Feelings of shame or "I deserve whatever I get" on the part of the victim
- Extreme dependency of one or both partners on the other
- Family history of battering or other violence

Child Abuse and Neglect

Abuse occurs when a physical or verbal action is taken against a child. Beating or berating or taking sexual advantage are some forms of child abuse. The deliberate failure to meet a child's basic needs constitutes neglect. Neglect may be emotional, physical, educational, or medical. No one knows exactly how many children are victimized in these ways by parents or primary caregivers. Abuse and neglect cases are underreported, in part because extended family, friends and professionals fail to notify authorities of their suspicions. In many areas of the country, numbers of reported cases have risen dramatically in the past decade. In a great many of these situations, the abusers have been found to have drug or alcohol histories (see Figure 2.2).

The precise causes of child battering are unknown. It has been suggested that in order for child abuse to occur three elements must be present:

1. There must be an adult capable of perpetrating violence.
2. The child must be perceived as "different" in some ways from his caregiver or family.
3. There must be a triggering event that culminates in the abuse.

This event does not have to be significant in the eyes of others, only to the abuser. For example, a toileting accident or a broken dish might lead to an abusive incident (see Figure 2.3).

The characteristics of families that are abusive of their children have undergone extensive study. Research indicates that parents who batter their children were often themselves victimized in childhood. In addition, these adults were frequently witnesses to other forms of family violence and discord. As adults, persons who abuse their children lack the maturity for healthy adult relationships and for effective childrearing. They are usually without support systems critical for effective parenting.

An unwanted pregnancy can be at the root of child abuse and neglect. For that parent, the all-important bond with the infant may fail to develop. A parent or caregiver's perception of the child as "different" also influences the instance of abuse and neglect. A child can be unlike his or her family by virtue of appearance, disability, or similarity to someone who has fallen out of favor with relatives.

Child abuse and neglect can occur in families of every economic, social and ethnic group. Poverty is a feature in many, but not all situations. Low income, unemployment, poor housing, and other deprivations are often found in families where abuse is pervasive.

Figure 2.2
Signs and Symptoms of Child Abuse and Neglect

- Unusual or unexplained bruises, welts, burns or fractures
- Bite marks
- Frequent emergency room visits
- Extreme withdrawal or acting-out behavior
- Overly affectionate behavior exhibited toward strange adults
- Lack of clean or weather-appropriate clothing
- Frequently stained or soiled underclothes
- Presence of sexually transmitted disease
- Stealing or hoarding food
- Unattended medical needs
- Irregular school attendance
- Unpleasant body odor
- Showing fear of parents or other adults
- Showing no distress at separation from or interest in reunion with parents

Figure 2.3
The Professional Response to Suspected Child Abuse or Neglect

---

- Document any signs or symptoms of abuse or neglect.
- Consult with appropriate colleagues or team members to share information or validate suspicions.
- Where appropriate, question the parent or guardian of the child in question.
- Report the abuse or neglect incident to the appropriate authorities in your area.
- Keep all information confidential.

Few methodological studies of the relationship between drug and alcohol addiction and child abuse and neglect have been conducted; however, poor parental health and substance abuse have both been linked to child victimization. In one nationwide study of 900,000 founded cases, 675,000 involved an adult who used drugs or alcohol. It is estimated that between 30 percent and 90 percent of all substantiated child abuse and neglect cases in the United States and three-quarters of the child fatalities in some cities involve adult substance abuse (4).

In spite of the speculation and some evidence supporting a link between addiction and child abuse, it has not been established as a cause. Rather substance abuse appears to be one of the many characteristics of abusing parents. In fact, in at least one study, women who use drugs were found to be less likely to use severe violence as a form of punishment (5). These same women may, however, neglect their children's emotional or physical needs.

Conversely, both physical and sexual abuse have been identified as possible factors in the development of substance-abuse problems, particularly among women. When studies revealed that a large percentage of females in recovery had been abuse and assault victims, researchers began exploring the possibility that these experiences were among the triggers of addiction (6). There are indications that low self-esteem, social isolation, and the need to repress unpleasant feelings and memories can lead an individual to medicate the pain with drugs and alcohol.

THE CHILD WELFARE RESPONSE

Over the years there have been many responses to the child abuse problem. Initially, abusive parents were thought to be entitled to discipline their children in whatever ways they deemed suitable. Later, all abusers were seen as evil, and it was thought best to separate their children from them, often permanently. Children were placed in residential care facilities or foster care homes. Parents were sometimes asked to voluntarily relinquish their children for adoption; in other cases their children were forcibly taken from them. In any event, few children were adopted.

In recent years the focus has shifted to family preservation. New approaches to treating child and parents have been developed. These include supporting the family through in-home services, and some residential programs for both mothers and their children. In-home services involve support from a trained home-based worker for the development of both parenting and homemaking skills. The family may also be required to participate in programs at a local community center.

Residential treatment programs provide 6 to 24 months of service in a supervised setting. Parenting and homemaking competencies are developed, along with stress reduction and coping skills. Mothers may have opportunities for educational and vocational skills training. This type of environment also offers the mother respite from the constant stress of childrearing.

The courts sometimes place abused and neglected children in the care of relatives. This may be the least satisfactory of the responses, however. The child welfare system seldom investigates relatives carefully. Both child abuse and addiction tend to be intergenerational, so the child may be no safer with relatives than with the parents. Family conflicts, even custody battles, sometimes result from what was designed to be a temporary situation. Furthermore, the extended family may become privy to confidential information that a parent wanted to remain private.

Like addiction treatment options, none of those for child abuse and neglect is right for every family. Some parents require more intensive involvement and support from social services and therapists. Some parents are relatively high functioning, while others have lives complicated by substance abuse, mental health problems, or other mitigating circumstances. Finally, when foster or residential care of the child alone is employed, there is tremendous stress placed on the child by the ongoing series of separations from and reunions with parents. As we try to determine the most effective ways for responding to the needs of these families, social service systems are being faced with staggering budget and staffing cuts.

Health Issues

Substance abuse often affects the user's physical health and emotional well-being. Drugs and alcohol can influence the body by interfering with the functioning of the immune system. Windows of vulnerability are then opened for infection, chronic illness, and disease. The addict's lifestyle may involve risk-taking behaviors, including crimes perpetrated for the purpose of obtaining money for drugs (burglaries, assaults, and prostitution). These behaviors place the drug and alcohol user at risk for physical injury. Unprotected sexual activity increases exposure to the HIV virus and other sexually transmitted disease, while the sharing of needles among intravenous drug users also promotes AIDS transmission.

Distracted by their addictions, individuals who abuse drugs and alcohol are less apt to take care of their overall health and nutrition. The health of their children may also be neglected.

ACQUIRED IMMUNE DEFICIENCY SYNDROME (AIDS)

It has been called the "plague" of modern times and has created feelings of fear and loathing in many otherwise caring people. When the human immuno-deficiency virus (HIV) and resulting acquired immune deficiency syndrome (AIDS) first came to public attention in the 1980s, it was assumed that the disease was limited to homosexuals. At the time, they were the population most affected. As information about HIV transmission became more widely available, it was evident that anyone who indulged in certain behaviors could be at risk. AIDS can be transmitted through unprotected sexual activity, through contaminated blood, or through the sharing of needles used to inject drugs.

Contamination of the donor blood supply in the Unites States appears to have been brought under control. Other causes of AIDS are still prevalent, however. Many drug users engage in risk-taking behaviors including unprotected sex and needle sharing. According to the United State Public Health Service there were 80,691 cases of AIDS reported in 1994. Of these, nearly 32,000 cases are estimated to result from drug-related causes, including intravenous drug use and sex with a person who is an IV drug user (7).

Acquired immune deficiency syndrome is now one of the three leading causes of death for young adults 25 to 44 years. The rates of infection for women and minorities are rising, along with the instance of HIV infection in suburban and rural areas of the United States.

In adults, the symptoms of AIDS may not appear for as many as 10 years after HIV exposure. A person may look and feel healthy, while able to contaminate others with the virus. Some of the symptoms of AIDS include fever, diarrhea, weight loss, fatigue, swollen lymph glands, and yeast infections (see Figures 2.4, 2.5).

There are many issues faced by persons with HIV or AIDS diagnosis. The diagnosis itself is often shocking and sudden in the severity of its implications. There can be extreme fear of disclosure to friends, relatives, and co-workers, and the resulting isolation. When the infected person does reveal the disease he or she may indeed be shunned by friends and family. As the illness progresses, there is a corresponding loss of self-esteem and the need to cope with dramatic changes in physical and mental health conditions. When the person with HIV or AIDS is a parent with young children, there are child care and respite needs to be met. The parent may also have to plan for the future care of his or her children. Not the least of the impacts is the societal assumption that infected persons are bad and deserving of their fate.

The tragedy of AIDS extends beyond the loss of life. In the next decade an estimated 125,000 children will be orphaned by the consequences of the epidemic (8).

Pediatric AIDS

Acquired immune deficiency syndrome can also affect infants and young children. It is currently among the top ten causes of death for children 1 to 10 years. Between 1978 and 1993, an estimated 14,920 HIV-infected children were born in the United States. Ninety-two percent of children under 13 who contract the disease do so prenatally. In 1994, 1,017 new cases of AIDS were reported among children (9). While rates of infection for adults in general have dropped in the past few years, those for children have increased. Studies indicate that 20 percent to 30 percent of children born to HIV-infected mothers develop AIDS (10). Infection can occur in utero, through exposure to blood or vaginal fluids during labor and delivery, or through the ingestion of infected breast milk after birth.

If a newborn is at risk for HIV infection, the child is tested soon after birth. New treatments are constantly being developed, and it is not uncommon for the infected child to receive medication designed to boost the immune system and to offset infection. Unlike adults with HIV, however, children exposed to the virus generally develop and display symptoms throughout the course of their illness. This may be due to the fact that their bodies are in phases of enhanced development and growth.

Wasting or failure to thrive is one of the first health problems to appear in the child with HIV. The child does not achieve developmental milestones on schedule and shows lags in motor skills growth. Weight and height gains lag behind those of peers. In some children neurologic symptoms appear in the form of seizure disorders. Pneumonia and other forms of bacterial infection may set in.

A common bacterial infection in both children and adults with AIDS is *thrush*. It appears in the mouth as a series of white, yeast-like spots on the tongue and inside of the cheeks. It should be noted that many young and healthy babies develop thrush, especially when they are put to bed with bottles of milk or formula. In the child with AIDS, this infection is persistent and difficult to treat.

Swollen glands and diarrhea are also common problems. Infections of the brain (encephalopathy) or the liver (hepatitis) and kidney failure may also affect children with AIDS.

Since the diagnosis of the first cases of AIDS in children, concern has been expressed by parents and school officials about disease transmission in the classroom. Young children do mouth and share toys, bottles, food, and eating utensils. They soil diapers, clothing, and bedding with urine, feces, and vomitus. They incur injuries from falls and fights. Even in the face of all of these behaviors, the child with HIV or AIDS is at greater risk from classmates than they are from him or her. The weakened immune system may not protect the child from their germs and viruses. What may make them ill for a day or two can kill the child with HIV or AIDS.

The virus that causes AIDS can be kept at bay by simple precautions such as regular handwashing; proper disposal of diapers, tissues, and paper towels; and use of rubber gloves for treatment of wounds, diapering, and toileting assistance.

The prognosis for the baby with HIV infection is not easily made. Some children die in infancy, others appear more resistant to severe infection, remaining relatively healthy into childhood. While there is much to be learned about the course of the disease in children, the rate of eventual mortality is very high.

Figure 2.4

Signs and Symptoms of Acquired Immune Deficiency Syndrome

- FEVERS
- SWOLLEN GLANDS
- DIARRHEA
- WEIGHT LOSS
- YEAST INFECTIONS
- LOWERED T-CELL COUNT

Figure 2.5

AIDS Is Not Transmitted by

. . . using a toilet seat used by an infected person

. . . kissing an infected person

. . . eating or drinking from utensils used by an infected person

. . . hugging an infected person

. . . sitting alongside an infected person

. . . handling objects touched by an infected person

. . . bathing an infected person

. . . holding the hand of an infected person

. . . wiping away the tears of an infected person

. . . breathing the same air as an infected person

TUBERCULOSIS

Once called "consumption," tuberculosis (TB) was the leading cause of death in nineteenth- and early twentieth-century America. Those infected were snatched from their families and isolated in sanatoriums. By the 1950s, the development of new drugs and improvements in housing and overall health conditions made tuberculosis a disease of the past. In the early 1980s, however, cases once again began appearing in large numbers in eastern cities.

An airborne disease, tuberculosis is usually spread when an infected person coughs and microscopic bacteria, called myobacterium tuberculosis, are inhaled into the body. Many of those infected never actually develop active TB, because a healthy immune system prevents the bacteria from multiplying out of control. If, however, someone lives or works in close, poorly ventilated quarters, has an immune system weakened by disease or old age, or has poor or non-existent health care services, he or she is more vulnerable to tuberculosis infection.

Antitubercular drugs can easily cure the disease if the prescribed medicines are taken consistently over the specified period. The infected person must often take at least two medications over a period of six months or more. The newest outbreak of tuberculosis has been influenced by several unexpected factors. Many of those infected with TB in the 1990s are impoverished, already ill with other diseases, and have less access to health care. When the medications to treat TB are taken sporadically, the results are disastrous. Health care professionals have reported the development of several new drug-resistant strains of tuberculosis. These have emerged because intermittent treatment killed off only the weakest bacteria, leaving the rest to develop immunity to the ordinarily effective medications. The drug-resistant strains of TB have mortality rates as high as 70 percent (11).

A second factor in the recent spread of TB is the increase in substance abuse and the complications it produces. Many illicit drugs affect the user by weakening the immune system. The addict is more apt to become ill when exposed to bacteria and viruses. Intravenous drug use has contributed to the rates of AIDS infection, which ravages the immune system. A person already weakened by AIDS is extremely vulnerable when it comes to tubercular infection.

While the general population is not presently at high risk for this form of tuberculosis, concern is growing. Pharmaceutical companies, which had once stopped developing drugs to combat TB, are now investing in this effort. Federal and state governments are beginning to advocate awareness, to urge TB testing, and to fund research in this area.

Homelessness

As the United States entered a period of severe economic recession in the early 1980s, unemployment rates skyrocketed and the number of people living in poverty began a steady increase. Homelessness, a problem associated with large cities and specific populations, began to affect previously middle class individuals from all areas of the country. As with many other social problems, the exact number of homeless is unknown. The homeless include the displaced, the unemployed, the mentally ill, and many who are drug and alcohol dependent. Some of the homeless are elderly, and many are children. Some are ill with AIDS or other debilitating diseases.

According to some sources, persons with substance-abuse problems are the fastest growing group of homeless nationwide (12). While numbers vary from city to city, this has undoubtedly been a neglected group of displaced people. The media coverage of homelessness has focused on families that have fallen on hard times—in other words, a more acceptable group of *street people*. The stories of mentally ill and addicted homeless are not so popular.

Influencing the rise in the number of homeless substance abusers is the disappearance of drop-in missions, single-room-occupancy hotels, and low-rent apartments. These types of housing were lost when urban renewal and gentrification changed the face of many cities beginning in the 1960s.

Until 1987, the majority of addicted street persons were identified as alcoholics (13). The appearance of crack cocaine, however, significantly altered the composition of the homeless population. Those who use crack often squander their resources in an attempt to get funds for drugs. They may steal from relatives and friends, and eventually their overtaxed kinship ties are severed. These and other problems of addicts, including AIDS, can lead to life on the streets.

Facing myriad social, health, and legal dilemmas, those who are addicted and homeless seldom find programs to address all of their needs. Treatment facilities cannot always provide housing, while shelters rarely provide recovery services. In a climate of apathy toward the homeless and the addicted, and decreased funding for all human service programs, it is unlikely that monies to provide an adequate response are forthcoming.

CHILDREN WITHOUT HOMES

Only intermittent public attention has been paid to the children whose family situations have left them homeless. The voices of agencies that advocate for children's rights have been loud, but they have been overwhelmed by others that say, "We have done enough!"

The combined impact of parental addiction and familial homelessness is one that strikes deeply and perhaps permanently at a child. In addition to the chaotic lifestyles, risk-taking, and ineffectual parenting of many substance-abusing parents, the child may also be subject to abuse and neglect. When these situations are complicated by homelessness, the child may face greater risk of psychosocial impairment.

Having a home to go to, whether a house or an apartment, provides a child with a familiar environment and a sense of security. Even if some of his or her life is in turmoil, and primary caregivers are not always reliable, a space and toys of her or his own can be reassuring to a child. Without these things, the child of addicted parents may be rudderless.

Homelessness can also interfere with a child's participation in a stabilizing child care or school program. The child may avoid school because of lack of appropriate clothing. He or she may have no place to complete homework or projects or to put textbooks for safekeeping. At school the child may be ostracized by other children, even by adults. The substance-abusing and homeless parent may not be in a position to recognize or support the child's school needs. Involvement with the child care center or school program may be sporadic or nonexistent.

Incarceration

In 1990 there were more than one million arrests for drug-related crimes. Two-thirds of these were for possession of illicit substances (14). An even larger number of Americans are arrested each year for driving under the influence of alcohol. The number of those arrested on drug charges who are subsequently indicted and convicted has steadily been increasing.

The specific offense, the type and amount of drugs involved, and the previous history of the offender are taken into account during sentencing; however the federal government and many states have mandatory minimal sentences for many drug offenses. House arrest, sometimes combined with electronic monitoring, has been used in some cases since the mid 1980s.

When incarcerated, a drug offender may serve time in a local, state, or federal facility. In 1991, 20 percent of those in state prisons and more than 50 percent of persons serving in federal correctional facilities were incarcerated for drug-related offenses.

Few prisons have comprehensive drug treatment services. While many prisons will detoxify a drug- or alcohol-abusing person on admission, indications are that drugs are readily available behind bars. Addiction can even begin during incarceration, as a coping mechanism.

If the individual charged is a juvenile, the results of a conviction can be very different. In some states, a youngster arrested on drug charges faces a hearing, rather than a trial. If convicted, that child may be labeled "delinquent" and sentenced to a juvenile facility. In some cases "shock incarceration" is used for teen and young adult offenders, provided they are nonviolent (15). These are boot camp kinds of settings employing military discipline to build self-esteem and character. Results of these programs have been mixed, and long-term follow-up is needed to determine their effectiveness. However, drugs are also often available in these settings.

There are many additional issues for the incarcerated person and his or her family. Many addicts who are sentenced to prison terms are already estranged from their children and extended families. They became part of the drug-using community before going to jail, and many previously important aspects of life may have long since become inconsequential as substance abuse became the dominant force in their lives.

It has been argued that society is fed up with the consequences of the drug problem in the United States, and dealers and users alike should be locked up and the keys thrown away. Perhaps for some of those who deal drugs this is true.

There are, however, many incarcerated whose primary crime is possession and drug use. At present, via the judicial system, little is done to treat the addiction problem and prepare the individual to return to society. Mothers and fathers who go to prison leave partners and grandparents to rear their children. Ties to their children are severely disrupted, even permanently broken. Few facilities offer programs to enable incarcerated parents to spend quality time with their children, and many families are damaged beyond repair.

We do not mean to suggest that drug-related offenses should not be penalized. Consideration must be given, however, to a realistic preparation for life outside of prison and a return to family life. An alienated, addicted inmate is more apt to be a repeat offender.

In Conclusion

This chapter has scratched the surface of problems that substance abuse brings to individuals and to their families. Those who have suffered along with or because of an addicted person know all too well the emotional, and possibly physical scars that can be left behind. While substance abuse is a devastating social problem, consuming millions of dollars and countless hours of time to remedy, it is also a deeply human and personal tragedy for individuals and families. We strongly advocate that the broader scope of the addictions problem be considered, and that our legislators begin to recognize that perhaps the greatest disaster is to consider some of our citizens expendable.

Endnotes

1. Goode, E. "Till Death Do Them Part?" *U.S. News and World Report*, July 4, 1994, pp. 24–28.

2. Kantor, G.K., and M.A. Straus. "Substance Abuse as a Precipitant of Family Violence Victimization," *American Journal of Drug and Alcohol Abuse*, 15 (2), pp. 173–189.

3. Goldstein, P.J. "The Drugs/Violence Nexus: A Tripartite Conceptual Framework," *Journal of Drug Issues*, 15 (4), 1985, pp. 493–506.

4. Daro, D., and L. Mitchell. *Current Trends in Child Abuse Reporting and Fatalities. The Results of the 1989 Annual Fifty-State Survey*. Chicago, IL: National Committee for the Prevention of Child Abuse, March 2, 1990.

5. Miller, B.A. "The Interrelationship Between Alcohol and Drugs and Family Violence, " In De La Rosa, M., E.Y. Lambert and B. Gropper, *Drugs and Violence: Causes, Correlates and Consequences*, NIDA Research Monograph Number 103. Washington, DC: National Institute on Drug Abuse, 1991.

6. Ibid.

7. *HIV/AIDS Surveillance Report, 6 (2)*. Atlanta, GA: Centers for Disease Control and Prevention, December 1994.

8. National Institute of Health. *Surgeon General's Report to the American Public on HIV Infection and AIDS*. Rockville, MD: Centers for Disease Control and Prevention, Health Resources and Services Administration, June 1993.

9. *HIV/AIDS Surveillance Report, 6 (2)*. Atlanta, GA: Centers for Disease Control and Prevention, December 1994.

10. National Institute of Health. *Surgeon General's Report to the American Public on HIV Infection and AIDS*. Rockville, MD: Centers for Disease Control and Prevention, Health Resources and Services Administration, June 1993.

11. Cowley, G., M. Hager and E.A. Leonard. "A New Face for an Old Nemesis," *Newsweek*, December 2, 1991, p. 70.

12. Whitman, D., D. Friedman and L. Thomas. "The Return of Skid Row," *U.S. News and World Report*, January 15, 1990, pp 27–29.

13. Ibid.

14. Bureau of Justice Statistics. *Drugs, Crime and the Justice System*. Washington, DC: U.S. Department of Justice, December 1992, p. 158.

15. Ibid., p. 183.

Resources

Ackerman, R.J., and D. Graham. *Too Old to Cry, Too Hurt to Laugh: Abused Teens in America*. Bradenton, FL: Human Services Institute/Tab Books, 1990.

Anderson, G.R. (Ed.). *Courage to Care. Responding to the Challenge of Children with AIDS*. Washington, DC: Child Welfare League of America, 1990.

Caring for Someone with AIDS. Washington, DC: U.S. Department of Health and Human Services, Public Health Service, 1993.

Cicchetti, D., and V. Carlson (Eds.). *Child Maltreatment: Theory and Research on the Causes and Consequences of Child Abuse and Neglect*. New York: Cambridge University Press, 1989.

Fenner-McBride, L.A. AIDS: *Legal and Ethical Considerations: Health Care Providers at Risk*. Tucson, AZ: Carondelet Management Institute, 1993.

Hershowitz, J., M. Seck, and C. Fogg. *Substance Abuse and Family Violence: Identification of Drug and Alcohol Usage During Child Abuse Investigations*. Boston, MA: Department of Social Services, June 1989.

Kempe, H., and R. Helfer. *The Battered Child*, Third Edition. Chicago, IL: University of Chicago Press, 1981.

McCarroll, T. *Morning Glory Babies: Children with AIDS and the Celebration of Life*. New York: St. Martin's Press, 1988.

McKenzie, N.F. (Ed.). *The AIDS Reader: Social, Political and Ethical Issues*. New York: Meridian Books, 1991.

Meeting the Challenge of HIV Infection in Family Foster Care. Washington, DC: Child Welfare League of America, 1990.

Mofenson, L. *Preventing Mother to Infant HIV Transmission: What We Know So Far*. The AIDS Reader, March/April 1992.

National Commission on AIDS. *The Twin Epidemics of Substance Abuse and HIV*. Washington, DC: National Commission on AIDS, 1991.

National Court Appointed Special Advocates Association. "Born into Addiction," *The Connection*, 5, Fall 1989, pp. 1–5.

Pernanem, K. "Alcohol and Crimes of Violence." In Kissin, B., and H. Begleiter. *The Biology of Alcoholism. Vol. 4, Social Aspects*. New York: Plenum Press, 1976, pp. 351–444.

Polansky, N.A., et al. *Child Neglect: Understanding and Reaching the Parent*. Washington, DC: Child Welfare League of America, 1972.

Preventing Child Abuse: A Resource for Policymakers and Advocates. Boston, MA: Massachusettes Committee for Children and Youth, 1987.

Regan, D.O., S.M. Ehrlich and L. Finnegan. "Infants of Drug Addicts: At Risk for Child Abuse and Neglect and Placement in Foster Care," *Neurotoxicology and Teratology*, 9, 19, pp. 315–319.

Rieder, I. and P. Ruppert (Ed.). *AIDS: The Women*. Cleis Press, 1988.

Serving Children with HIV Infection in Child Day Care: A Guide for Center-Based and Family Day Care Providers. Washington, DC: Child Welfare League of America, 1991.

Sorenson, J.L., et al. *Preventing AIDS in Drug Users and Their Sexual Partners*. New York: Guilford Press, 1991.

TB/HIV: The Connection: What Health Care Workers Should Know. Washington, DC: U.S. Department of Health and Human Services, Public Health Service, 1993.

Tonry, M. and J.Q. Wilson (Eds.). *Drugs and Crime*. Vol. 13, *Crime and Justice*. Chicago, IL: University of Chicago Press, 1990.

CHAPTER THREE

Drug Abuse and Parenting

No one knows the exact toll taken by substance abuse on children. We are certain that many children are born prenatally exposed to drugs, while others become substance abusers themselves. In between these two very serious problems are the children who live every day with the impact of parental drug and alcohol abuse. We know, too that these children are more apt to become victims of physical or sexual abuse or neglect, and often come under the jurisdiction of the child welfare system.

When parents are serious drug users, they typically do not adequately care for their children. Many of these children are taken in by grandparents or other relatives. Others must be cared for by the social service system (1).

As detailed in Chapter Two, the characteristics of substance abusers include low self-esteem and the frequency with which they come from families where addiction, family violence, and other forms of interpersonal dysfunction were already problems (2). In other words, the substance-abusing parent often lacked models for parenting and positive childhood experiences on which to draw. Adding fuel to this deadly mix is the fact that pregnancy among users is often unplanned and unwanted; however, by the time the woman is aware that she is with child, the pregnancy is significantly advanced.

In this chapter we will look at how the precursors of addiction and its psychosocial consequences influence the ability to parent. We will also examine the growth of parenting competence during the addictions-recovery process.

The Effects of Childhood Experiences on Parenting

Two decades ago, when Selma Fraiberg studied parent-child relationships, she documented the influence of childhood traumas on later parenting (3). Fraiberg and her colleagues recognized that emotional deprivation, physical abuse and neglect, and maternal apathy were among the contributing factors when women later failed to develop nurturing behaviors.

More recently, research has highlighted a pattern among those affected by chemical dependence that includes these factors along with ". . . parental death and/or desertion, divorce, marital disharmony, poor parental role modeling, parental substance abuse, and high rates of . . . sexual abuse . . ." (4)

These striking features of the addictive experience play a profound role in developing parenting skills. For example, John Bowlby (renowned theorist on parent-child attachment relations) has described the child's strong dependence on a primary attachment figure (5). This parent or chief caregiver must be a positive and regular presence in the life of the child, contributing to a sense of stability and must, in Erikson's terms, build in the child a sense of "basic trust." The child who experiences a loss or separation from this key figure in his or her life without loving support, may reach grownup life lacking the ability to form close interpersonal relationships—always fearing that loved ones will go away. Similarly, parental divorce and family breakup impact on the child by challenging the child's sense of self and worthiness of love and care by others.

The lack of positive role models for parenting also plays a crucial role in the breakdown of parenting skills. Children learn nurturing and compassion through loving care by others. The binding up of scraped knees and bruised feelings is as important an aspect of parenting as the use of resources to feed, clothe, and shelter a child. The failure to comfort the injured child, to lovingly cuddle, to demonstrate forgiveness for the tiny infractions of childhood can produce another unyielding, unforgiving, and apathetic parent when adulthood is reached.

Physical and sexual abuse wreak havoc on a developing psyche. The child suffers untold wounds, both physical and emotional. Many become conflicted in a damaging love-hate relationship with the abusing parent (6). On one hand, they may believe they deserve the abuse, have done something to deserve it. They may work harder to win parental approval only to find that the abuse continues or increases. Consequently, anger and hostility grow toward the offending parent and others who fail to protect the child from the abuse. The child may fail to develop skills necessary for successful relationships.

Even without the complication of addiction, the groundwork is laid through these early experiences for parenting problems. With the addition of the substance-abuse factor, parenting is doomed to dysfunction and breakdown.

The Role of Addiction

There are many aspects of substance abuse and its consequences that contribute to parenting problems. Becoming a mother or father, from the outset, demands a degree of selflessness; the parent must focus on the needs of the child. In turn, parent-child attachment grows in part out of caregiving experiences and the sense of satisfaction that evolves as one successfully recognizes and responds to the needs of the child (7). By contrast, the addicted parent is focused on the need to obtain and use drugs or alcohol. The physical and psychological needs that accompany addiction can supersede all else.

Furthermore, there are aspects of the addict's lifestyle that interfere with effective parenting. These include a high instance of poverty,[*] inadequate education, poor coping skills, and a lack of social support systems (8). All of these have been positively correlated with increased rates of child abuse and neglect (9). The substance-abusing parent is usually surrounded by other members of the addictions community. There are few positive role models or success stories, no one in whom to observe the day-to-day struggles of effective parenting. It was this lack of sources for modeling that caused Fraiberg to move therapist/parent educators into the homes of dysfunctional mother-child dyads, in order for parenting to be taught and learned step by step.

---

[*] It should be noted again that substance abuse can occur in any socioeconomic group.

Chemically dependent women are known to have strong, stereotypic beliefs about female roles, and to have corresponding feelings of inadequacy and inability to control their lives (10). These are not emotions that yield positive responses to parenting, or feelings that one can significantly influence the lives of her children.

The Role of the Substance-Exposed Infant

It may seem harsh to suggest that newborns or young children influence the way that their parents treat them. In truth, they do play a role, albeit an involuntary one. The egocentric nature of infants and children keeps them from the realization that constant demands for food, clean clothing, and comfort are tiring even for a high functioning, healthy parent. To an addicted parent, these may represent demands that simply cannot be met.

Further complicating this relationship are the physiologic and behavioral characteristics of infants experiencing neonatal abstinence syndrome. The baby who must withdraw from drugs prenatally introduced into his or her system may exhibit feeding and digestion problems and frequent stretching (that may be mistaken for physical rigidity), and may be difficult to comfort (11). Thus, at the very time that the parent needs to experience success and satisfaction in attempts to care for the newborn, she may feel thwarted, even rejected by the baby.

It is not unusual for parents to blame themselves for either real or imagined problems of their children. This is particularly true of addicted parents. The feelings of guilt are often profound, and yet they can actually influence increased drug use as a coping mechanism.

The Growth of Parenting Skills During Recovery

A decade ago, in studying attachment, the authors first understood the resilience of the parent-child relationship. It is an astounding feature of human development and interaction that even when stretched to the limits of endurance, relationships can sometimes be restored to a healthy level of functioning.

Contributing to the potential for growth and change among addicted parents is the degree of love and devotion to their children often exhibited by women in treatment programs. In fact, presence in treatment is often motivated by pregnancy and the existence of older children.

What follows is a description of the changes observed in women recovering from heroin and cocaine addiction as they progress through a series of stages that denote growth in parenting competence. While these ideas have not resulted from empirical research, they do represent three years of intense interaction with parents and their children in a comprehensive substance abuse treatment program.

A TREATMENT PROGRAM OVERVIEW

The treatment program under discussion is located in an eastern metropolitan area. While receiving funds from a variety of outside sources, the program is under the umbrella of a large medical research and training facility. Only women are treated. They enter the treatment program voluntarily, the chief admission criteria being pregnancy and addiction.

The women tend to be in their late 20s or early 30s in age, usually have several other children, and may have had previous, unsuccessful experiences with treatment. Most of the women have a drug of choice (heroin or cocaine), but have also experimented with other drugs, including alcohol. The average onset of drug usage is 12 years of age.

THE PARENT-CHILD CENTER

The Parent-Child Center component of this program, developed by one of the authors, included individual parent counseling and parent support groups, developmental groups for children aged birth through school age, and parent and child workshops. The focus of work with parents was the teaching of parenting skills, while helping parents deal with day-to-day childrearing crises.

While in the recovery process, parents were found to experience many setbacks and relapses. The causes may or may not be related to parenting, but parenting is always affected. The women also had high rates of depression and other affective disorders. These were shown to be related to continued drug use and problems attaching to their infants (12, 13).

Work with a Parent-Child Specialist, however, and a team of other staff that included social worker/therapists, and health care and psychiatric professionals yielded changes over time as recovery progressed.

Stages in the Growth of Parenting Competence (14)

STAGE 1—THE SUBSTANCE-ABUSING PARENT

Characteristics of the Mother

As previously stated, the substance-abusing woman is egocentric. Her focus is on meeting her own needs, particularly with regard to obtaining drugs and/or alcohol. It was also found that addicted women appear to have some psychosocial development fixation that correlates with their early adolescent onset of drug use. Their poor social and daily living skills are not unlike those of teenagers, and there is a corresponding lack of impulse control. The tendency of the mother at this stage is to repeat any abusive or neglectful patterns of her own childhood, for she does not recognize them as such. Her addiction is often kept hidden from family and friends.

Impact on the Child

While the child's mother still regularly uses drugs, there is a far greater risk of child abuse and neglect. Infants of addicted mothers may have some temporary motor delays, in addition to evidencing symptoms that appear related to neonatal abstinence syndrome. Older children may demonstrate social and language delays.

It must be emphasized that most delays appear to be related to the atmosphere for development created by substance abuse, rather than by prenatal drug exposure; that is, the mother's inability to provide a growth-enhancing environment is the apparent cause of many lags in development.

Roles for Human Service Professionals

Those working with actively substance-abusing women are generally regarded with mistrust and suspicion. Previous experience with the social services system has taught these women that outsiders may be a threat to them, especially where their children and notification of child protective services is concerned. These parents are difficult but not impossible to reach. This stage should be viewed as one of acquaintance and beginning a relationship. Threats related to the inadequacy of child care and rearing may result in a parent's flight and inaccessibility.

STAGE 2—FIRST SHORT PERIOD OF SOBRIETY AND/OR METHADONE MAINTENANCE

Characteristics of the Mother

In Stage 2, the mother continues to be egocentric, but improvement in her impulse control may be evident. Consequently, she may indicate the need to begin structuring her life and to create some degree of consistency for herself and her children. The first indicator of this change might be regular appearance at appointments and treatment sessions. Her awareness of her children's needs may be growing, although it is usually limited and is sometimes confused with her own emotional needs.

A drawback at this stage is the possibility of parent-child enmeshment—an unhealthy overattachment. We have likened this to replacing drug addiction with addiction to the child. This mother, who has been able at last to fall in love with her child, relishes their love affair and the child's need for and dependence on her. Thus, milestones that may indicate the child's normal development may be perceived by the addicted mother as threatening.

One mother had been urged to allow her nine-month-old to play with kitchen pots and stirring spoons. As she bent over to play with him, he playfully struck her on the head with a pot, much as he had been hitting the pots with the wooden spoons. Several days later she appeared at the treatment center in a distraught and tearful state. She recounted the incident with the pot and proclaimed, "He's going to grow up and beat me, just like all the other men in my life!"

Impact on the Child

At this stage the child's developing self-esteem and autonomy may be threatened, if the parent is unable to see the child as a separate being. The separation-individuation process that should take place in a healthy infancy is not permitted to develop. Overindulgence of children with an emphasis on toys and clothing and permissive scheduling is common.

Roles for Human Service Professionals

The beginning of sobriety provides a window of opportunity for the growth of trust in the relationship of the helper with the parent. General discussion of specific problems raised by the parent can be attempted, although care should be taken not to overwhelm the parent with the scope of her maternal role and the need for change. Some nurturing of this adult by a trusted professional can help to raise levels of self-esteem and awareness. Caution is urged, however, in this area as well, for over attachment to a helping professional is commonplace.

STAGE 3—RELAPSE PERIOD

Characteristics of the Mother

Unfortunately, relapse is common in the recovery process. There are many possible reasons for this, among them a lack of familiarity with success experiences. When relapse occurs, however, it means a return to the previous addictive behaviors for an undetermined period. Sometimes relapse lasts for just a few days—at other times for weeks or months. This time, however, drug use is accompanied by significant feelings of guilt—guilt for the failure to remain sober and guilt for the impact that the relapse has on herself and on her children.

If there is involvement with an early childhood program or specialist, the mother may even express resentment for the attentions paid to her child. In her overidentification with the child, she sees him as "good," while she is "bad" for relapsing. As one mother expressed her feelings, "*He* (the child) gets more attention around here than I do!"

Impact on the Child

Even infants younger than a year old have been observed to react to maternal drug relapse. Babies' responses may include increased fretfulness, eating problems, even illness. Older children, however, often demonstrate regressive or acting-out behavior. They may become significantly less cooperative in their interactions with adults. Strikingly, boys were found to show more aggressive and angry behaviors, while girls tended to withdraw and turn emotions inward.

Roles for Human Service Professionals

Some success in approaching the mother about ways to meet her child's needs may be possible. Helping persons should avoid increasing parental guilt. Connecting with the mother about specific techniques for helping her child to cope may be a workable strategy, while playing the role of a temporary stability figure for the child.

STAGE 4—RENEWED SOBRIETY

Characteristics of the Mother

While the return of sobriety following relapse should be seen as positive, it is not a phase without drawbacks. The woman may be convinced that she has finally "made it," only to later experience another relapse and the accompanying depression. At this time she may make her first attempt to separate herself socially from the addictions/ recovery communities. Rather than seeing herself as recovering, she may assume a stance that suggests, "I'm not like *them*." She may suddenly see herself as having vastly improved parenting skills, even offering advice to other parents.

She does not yet accept the long-term consequences of her addiction. In her efforts to be a clean and sober individual, she continues to hide her addiction from some family members and friends.

Impact on the Child

One of the more disturbing aspects of maternal recovery may be observed at this stage, when the mother may emotionally separate her children into two groups. One group we call the "children of addiction." These are the children born while the mother was actively using drugs or alcohol. She may view the individual child as "soiled" by her addiction, often expressing a high degree of dissatisfaction with that child, who may be incapable of pleasing her. If this child carries anger toward the parent for abuse or neglect offenses, their relationship may be further complicated by accusations and the child's learned mode of negative interaction.

The teenage son of one woman in recovery, knowing his mother's fear of exposure to the neighbors, would culminate their arguments by rushing into their yard and screaming at his mother, "You ____ heroin addict!"

The "children of recovery" are in equal jeopardy. This child, born after the start of the recovery process, is seen as being endowed with the grace of the mother's changing life. The child may not be permitted to make any mistakes, and is usually unable to meet overwhelming parental expectations.

One three-year-old often commented to her teachers that she was "not a good child." Unable to meet her mother's rigid toilet training schedule, the child withheld her feces to avoid soiling herself until hospitalization was required.

Roles for Human Service Professionals

This parent must be gradually helped to understand the lifelong nature of recovery, and that membership in this community is a positive and helpful one. At the same time, a period for serious child advocacy on the part of a helping professional has begun. Each child must be seen as individual and worthwhile, and techniques should be sought with the parent to meet children's individual needs. The parent may be more open to learning about the ways that expectations for her children can influence both positive and negative developmental outcomes. This parent can probably benefit from more intensive forms of parenting and parent-child therapy.

STAGE 5—TRUE SOBRIETY

Characteristics of the Mother

True sobriety is reached only as the woman achieves control over her drug problem while developing the capacity to deal openly and honestly with the consequences of addiction. She will begin to reveal her addiction to those from whom she has kept it secret, and may even discuss aspects of it with her older children. Maintaining sobriety will be at the top of her list of priorities. She understands that modeling her growing self-respect, self-esteem, and personal care for her children gives them permission to have positive feelings about, and to care for, themselves. The woman has a greater ability to make use of appropriate support systems. It is not unusual for a desire to counsel other addicted persons to be expressed. She focuses on continuing recovery and personal growth. She develops a more accurate view of her maternal strengths and weaknesses.

Impact on the Child

As the mother advances in her recovery, her children may have their first real opportunities to separate from her and to develop their own identities. With support they can come to terms with the past and may be able to reject patterns set by early parenting. A time for potentially healthy growth of the parent-child relationship has arrived.

Roles for Human Service Professionals

When this final stage has been reached the parent is more apt to have specific questions about parenting and to ask for support. The helping professional should be available to listen and to assist parents in making appropriate choices; however, stress should continue to be placed on strengthening maternal self-esteem and competence.

Figure 3.1
Stages in the Development of Parenting Competence in
the Substance-abusing woman

Stage	Characteristics of the Mother	Impact on the Child	Role of the Parent Educator
1 Drug-Abusing Mother	Egocentric; focused on own needs, in particular obtaining drugs/alcohol; little structure in daily life; few/no sober support systems; poor impulse control; tendency to repeat abusive/neglectful patterns of own childhood	May be victim of abuse/neglect; lags often apparent in language and social skills development	Usually viewed with mistrust, suspicion; woman is difficult to reach as parenting is not an issue
2 Short Period of Sobriety/ Methadone Maintenence	Continuing egocentrism; some impulse control improvement; developing awareness of need for life structuring, some awareness of child's needs; possibility of enmeshment, strong overidentification with child; child's developmental milestones may be perceived as threatening	May be parentified; develops awareness of parental dependence; self-esteem and autonomy are negatively affected; not viewed as an individual by parent	Growth of trust in relationship with woman; discussion of certain childrearing problems may be possible
3 Relapse Period	Behavior regression to Stage 1; significant guilt is experienced related to relapse and its effects; shows beginning-understanding of impact of addiction on self, child; may resent attentions to child; feel/express anger, resentment toward parent educator	Acting-out, regressive or withdrawn behaviors are common; aggression/ destructive behavior most obvious in boys; girls may turn emotions inward, withdraw	Discussion of child's needs may be possible; should be approached with caution to avoid overwhelming mother

Figure 3.1 (continued)
Stages in the Development of Parenting Competence in
the Substance-abusing woman

4 Renewed Sobriety	Woman becomes concerned with others' opinions of her/her child; wants to be seen as sober, not part of community of addicted persons; addiction may still be hidden from children/ extended family	May be viewed as "child of addiction" or "child of sobriety" (good vs. bad child); strong guilt feelings may develop as child is unable to meet parental expectations; child at high risk for emotional damage	Attempt to reach parent about dangers to child's psychosocial development; needs to be challenged to change parenting style/behaviors
5 True Sobriety	Woman able to deal more honestly with addiction issues; reveals addiction to children, extended family; focuses on change, personal growth; best able to use all appropriate support systems, including parent educator	Child has opportunity to separate from parent, develop own identity; chance to reject patterns set by early parenting; with support may experience catch-up period of development	Respond as needed to maternal overtures for feedback, support

The Voices of Fathers

The research on the psychosocial impacts of drug and alcohol abuse contains surprisingly little about fathers. Those who have studied the effects of substance abuse seem to indicate from their choice of topics that a man's ability to *produce* offspring is more critical than his capacity to rear them. Conversely, the literature on women and addictions is fraught with references to the effects on parenting. It takes, however, two adults to procreate, and children are generally aware of the existence of both parents, even when one is not present in the home. The absent parent can have as great a bearing on the child's social-emotional well-being as any custodial adult.

The authors believe that in spite of lack of attention to fathering the voices of fathers recovering from addiction should be heard. Men in a substance-abuse treatment program were surveyed in July 1995, and were asked to comment on the ways that addiction has affected relationships with their children. The small sample included fathers recovering from alcohol, cocaine and heroin addiction. Most were polydrug users. Their responses to the survey questions were voluntary.

Respondents said that being addicted to drugs and alcohol meant that they had no time for their children, "I was just worried about getting high." They indicated that substance abuse kept them from accepting responsibility for their children. Fathers said that their children were also affected by family violence and a lack of communication in their homes.

In the cases where the children knew of their parents' addiction, it was often the fathers themselves, or fathers and mothers together, who had told them.

The men also expressed a need to reunite with their children, in the many cases where there had been separations or estrangements, to be ". . . a real family." They indicated a desire to be a more positive influence on their children in the future. One father may have said it best by stating, "I would like to regain (my children's) full trust and respect."

Helping men to develop parenting skills and to become functioning members of their families is clearly a neglected area of substance-abuse research and treatment. There is much evidence to indicate that children who enjoy healthy father-child relationships benefit psychosocially and cognitively. Recovering fathers need the assistance of parenting and child development specialists to reach out and build relationships with their children, to learn that it is never too late to be a good father.

In Conclusion

The characteristics of addiction and stages in the growth of parenting competence will not be observed in every using and/or recovering parent. They are meant to provide a framework for viewing the family in the context of substance abuse. We stress that helping mothers, fathers, and children overcome the effects of substance abuse is not the role of one professional, but is that of a team. There is no one field that currently combines expertise in addictions, treatment, health and psychosocial implications, prenatal and antenatal effects on children, and impact on the overall family. Therefore, human service professionals must work together, ask questions, and seek answers for the benefit of parent and child.

Fathering Survey

Please answer the questions below to the best of your ability. If you are uncomfortable with any question, skip it and go on to the next one. If you do not have enough space to answer any question, use the back of the survey for additional comments.

Your age: _____   Your ethnic group: _____

Your drug of choice: _____

Length of time in treatment: _____

Number of children you have: _____   Ages of children: _____

Do you usually live with your children? _____

If not, what types of contact do you have with them (regular visits, telephone, mail)?

_____

_____

Do you feel that your addiction has changed your relationship with your children ? If so, in what ways?

_____

_____

Do your children know that you are recovering from addiction? If so, how did they find out?

_____

_____

Did addiction affect the way you thought about being a father? If so, in what ways?

_____

_____

Has recovery and treatment affected the way you feel about being a father? If so, in what ways?

_____

_____

In the future, what kinds of changes would you like to see in your relationship with your children?

_____

_____

Endnotes

1. *A National Report: Drugs, Crime and the Justice System.* Washington, DC: U.S. Department of Justice, December 1992, p. 9.

2. Davis, S.K. "Chemical Dependencey in Women: A Description of Its Effects and Outcomes on Adequate Parenting," *Journal of Substance Abuse Treatment* (7), 1990, pp. 226–227.

3. Fraiberg, S., E. Adelson, and V. Shapiro. "Ghosts in the Nursery: A Psychoanalytic Approach to the Problems of Impaired Infant-Mother Relationships," *Journal of the American Academy of Child Psychiatry.* (14), 1975, pp. 387–421.

4. Chambers, C.D., R.K. Hinesby, and M. Moldestad. "Narcotic Addiction in Females: A Race Comparison," *International Journal of the Addictions* (5), 1970, pp. 257–278.

5. Bowlby, J. *Attachment and Loss.* Vols I-III. New York: Basic Books, 1969, 1973, 1980.

6. Ibid.

7. Main, M. and J. Stadtman. "Infant Response to Rejection of Physical Contact By the Mother," *Journal of the American Academy of Pediatrics* (20), 1981, pp. 292–307.

8. Davis, S.K., "Chemical Dependence in Women: A Description of Its Effects and Outcome on Adequate Parenting," *Journal of Substance Abuse Treatment* (7), 1990, p. 225.

9. Kempe, R.S. and H.C. Kempe. *Child Abuse.* Cambridge, MA: Harvard University Press, 1978.

10. Weiner, B. (Ed.). *Achievement Motivation and Attribution Theory.* Morristown, NJ: General Learning Press, 1974.

11. Kaltenbach, K., and L.P. Finnegan. "The Influence of the Neonatal Abstinence Syndrome on Mother-Infant Interaction," In E.J. Anthony and C. Chiland (Eds.), *The Child and His Family: Perilous Development, Child Raising and Identity Formation Under Stress*, Vol. 8. New York: Wiley-Interscience, 1988.

12. Finnegan, L.P., S.M. Ohlberg, D. O'Malley and M.E. Rudrauff. "Evaluation of Parenting, Depression and Violence Profiles in Methadone Maintained Women," In *Child Abuse and Neglect*, Vol. 5, 1981, pp. 267–273.

13. Focus is placed on parenting women because the literature contains little on male substance abuse and parenting.

14. Presented at the Fifth Annual Conference on "Issues in Infancy," Allegheny General Hospital, Pittsburgh, PA, October 14, 1993.

CHAPTER FOUR

Drugs, Alcohol, and Children

Beginning in the late 1980s, news magazines, television programs, and professional journals began sounding a warning that a new breed of children was being born. Exposed to harmful substances in the womb, the children of drug addicts were described as prone to violence, emotionless, and beyond most interventions. In addition, they were supposedly characterized by physical and cognitive deficits of unknown extent. These images have been deeply imprinted in the minds of the public and have affected even those education, health, and human service professionals that come into contact with families.

In this chapter we will attempt to separate myth from fact. While keeping in mind that research is ongoing, we will address some central questions about prenatal drug exposure. How do drugs and alcohol affect the fetus and infant? What types of known effects are long- versus short-term? What is the structure of effective intervention for substance-exposed children and their families? What factors should be considered when working with parents and other primary caregivers?

Although much of what is described in the following pages may sound frightening, it will also become apparent that long-term outcomes are significantly less foreboding than we have been led to believe—especially with regard to cocaine and opiate use.

"Shadow Children:" The Crack Baby Myth

The initial wave of crack babies, born after crack cocaine hit the streets in the mid 1980s, are kindergarten age today. The arrival of those first afflicted youngsters in the public schools marks the beginning of a struggle that will deplete educational resources and test the compassion of public school educators. (1)

So the warnings were sounded. The former director of the National Center on Child Abuse called cocaine-exposed children a potential "bio-underclass." (2) He suggested that factors like economic disadvantage and physiologic damage would place the children in a category of permanent inferiority (see Figure 4.1).

A cadre of well-respected medical professionals and journalists were among the doomsayers. So what has been wrong with their pronouncements? A great deal about the early reports, it turns out, has been misleading. Researchers are still uncovering the full impact of cocaine exposure on the fetus and newborn. The entire picture may be unclear for several more decades; however, the initial reports of the effects of cocaine exposure were certainly exaggerated.

When reporting news stories, the media tend to take an oversimplified and emotional stance. A dramatic portrait is often painted; it is not unusual to present the worst-case scenarios, in which key factors may have been overlooked or omitted.

Even medical researchers sometimes fail to take certain variables into account. In the case of children prenatally exposed to cocaine, there were several significant issues that were not fully explored when research was first conducted. For example, when predicting that cocaine causes birth defects or congenital anomalies, it was generally not known whether mothers or fathers of the children already carried the recessive genes that produce some disorders. Drug-addicted women are prone to an avoidance of prenatal care. At times, drug use interferes with proper care of their bodies and unborn babies. They may wish to avoid detection of their addiction that might occur under the care of a physician. Prenatal testing or other health care that can identify or offset the occurrence of infant health problems is, therefore, lacking.

A second problem of early studies was their failure to account for mothers' polydrug use; that is, persons who abuse drugs often use more than one drug simultaneously. So, while studying cocaine-addicted women, researchers did not always ascertain whether other drugs or alcohol were also involved. While the effects of cocaine and opiate drugs are still in question, the impact of prolonged alcohol exposure is not. Some research aimed at cocaine abuse clearly yielded results that were linked to alcohol use.

Figure 4.1
Myths About Prenatally Drug-Exposed Children

- They have physical malformations and congenital anomalies.
- They have unalterable cognitive deficits.
- They lack normal emotions and are psychologically damaged.
- They are prone to violence.
- They are beyond professional help.

The third of this series of research issues is related to the length of time that crack cocaine has been in widespread use in the United States. While educational journals and news magazines were busy reporting an epidemic of crack babies in the nation's classrooms, the first group of cocaine-exposed children were still in diapers. Those children are only now reaching school age. To date, there has been insufficient longitudinal research to determine what the cocaine-exposed child faces in later childhood or adolescence.

It must also be said that research does not support that cocaine-exposed babies are born "addicted." (3) Immediately after birth they do show a series of symptoms related to drug exposure in the womb. This is a vast difference from being born with a craving for cocaine, as some studies suggest. Nor is there evidence to support the idea that prenatal drug exposure is a predictor of addiction in adult life.

It is interesting that after nearly a decade of cover and front page stories on the specter of the crack baby, when new research showed a different set of outcomes they were made public in far less dramatic forms. The April 20, 1992 issue of *Newsweek* contained a one-column article on page 75 of its "Health" section. This article cited a report in the *Journal of Neurotoxicology and Teratology*, a leader in research on those substances affecting the fetus. This study examined the impact of cocaine, cigarette, and alcohol use by pregnant women. In this case polydrug use was fully accounted for. Results of this research showed that cocaine had less of an impact on newborn behavior than either alcohol or smoking. Furthermore, this study indicated that the crack baby syndrome, so often described in other research, could be largely accounted for by low birth weight. Cocaine *does* interfere with a woman's ability to carry her baby to term.

In bringing these issues to light, we do not mean to suggest that any form of drug use is acceptable. Substance abuse is among the most serious of American social problems. An unfounded, hysterical reaction, however, is not in the interest of the family or of society. What is most helpful to both addicted parents and to their drug-exposed children is an educated and compassionate public.

Cocaine: The Known Effects

The number of prenatally substance-exposed infants is unknown. To have some idea how many babies are exposed in utero, some form of mandatory testing of delivering mothers would be necessary. At present, some hospitals test all mothers-to-be, some test on the basis of physician recommendation, and some rely on women's self-reporting of drug use.

The National Institute on Drug Abuse (NIDA) conducts regular surveys of substance abuse among a cross-section of American families. While results of the 1990 survey do not include a separate report of drug use among pregnant women, the information available is nonetheless telling. Birth rates are the highest for women in the 18–34-year age group. This is the same period during which both cocaine and alcohol use are at their peak. Of those women responding to the 1990 NIDA survey, 4.5 percent admitted to cocaine use and 73 percent to alcohol use (4). Interestingly, women were not questioned about their use of opiates, although heroin use among women is a serious problem (see Figure 4.2). Other research studies have looked at drug use among pregnant women in specific geographic areas of the country—such as those with high population density. One such study found that delivering women at the Boston City Hospital had cocaine use rates of 18 percent (5).

The specific effects of cocaine use on the newborn appear to be dependent on a series of factors (6). The stage of gestation in which the fetus is exposed to the drug plays a role. Two-thirds of the problems that the baby develops in utero result from exposure to teratogens (substances that negatively affect the fetus) in the first three months of the pregnancy. The amount of the drug consumed by the mother is also a factor. Some women are experimenters, while others use many times daily. It is suggested that there are also unknown genetic influences at work that make some infants more vulnerable to maternal drug use. Thus, we see some babies less affected, while others incur more adverse reactions, although their mothers used a similar amount of the drug.

Yet another factor is an enzyme at work in the mother's body. Cholinesterase metabolizes cocaine by breaking down the compounds that make up the drug so the body can use it more effectively. In some pregnant women, cholinesterase levels are increased, in others decreased, and in a third group they remain unchanged from a non-pregnant state. So the amount of the drug affecting the baby is also influenced by the level of metabolizing enzyme present in the mother.

Cocaine reaches the fetus by "crossing the placenta," that is, by entering the mother's bloodstream and being transmitted to the baby in the same way that nutrients from the mother's food supply reach the fetus.

Many initial adverse effects have been reported, although not all have been based on systematically conducted research. Substantive studies exist to support the finding that cocaine use influences the size of the baby at birth and the circumference of the baby's head. A smaller head size can mean a restriction of brain growth and development. Intrauterine growth retardation is thought to be a result of the constriction of blood vessels. These same blood vessels transport nutrients to the fetus, and the baby's size is reduced. Cocaine-exposed infants were found by one researcher to average nearly a pound less in birth weight than nonexposed children (7). It should be noted that lower birth weight can also be caused by other teratogens, such as cigarette smoking, marijuana use, and alcohol abuse. Poor nutrition is also a factor with small-for-date babies. Each of these is among the characteristic behaviors of cocaine-abusing women.

Low birth weight is also associated with conditions known to have a profound affect on child development. Intraventricular hemorrhages (IVH), or the bleeding of blood vessels in the brain, is a not uncommon problem of premature and low-birth-weight babies. The outcomes of IVH include cerebral palsy, seizure disorders, central nervous system damage, and even mental retardation (8).

Among the most frequently documented of the effects of maternal cocaine use are increased muscle tone, sleeping and eating problems, and difficulty being soothed. Increases in muscle tone may appear as tenseness or stretching behavior. While being held the baby may be unable to relax into the parent or caretaker's body, unless deeply asleep. This can cause a great deal of frustration for a new mother, who perceives her child to be noncuddly or rejecting.

Similar feelings on the part of the mother may arise when the infant feeds poorly. The baby may seem to gulp, then choke on formula, resulting in the frequent need to be patted and soothed before beginning to eat again. Giving a bottle may seem like a major ordeal, rather than ideal moments for parent-child acquaintance.

Figure 4.2
Known Effects of Prenatal Drug and Alcohol Exposure

	Cocaine	*Opiates*	*Alcohol (FAS/FAE)*
At Birth	low birth weight; small head circumference; increased muscle tone; sleeping and eating disorders; hard to comfort	low birth weight; small head circumference; increased muscle tone; sleeping and eating disorders; neonatal abstinence syndrome (decreased attentional abilities/ social responsiveness; heightened sensitivity to various stimuli; exaggerated reflexes; stuffy/runny nose; rapid respirations; apnea; chest contractions	low birth weight; small head circumference; craniofacial malformations (small eyes/eye openings; malformed ears; poorly defined philtrum; thin upper lip/nose; flattened midfacial features; crossed eyes); heart murmurs; kidney/liver problems; undescended testicles; hernias; increased muscle tension; sleep problems; hard to comfort; reflex abnormalities; mental retardation
In Childhood	*Toddler:* lower scores on measures of development; less appropriate play; more impulsive; less securely attached *Preschooler:* most test normally on developmental/language/behavioral tests; some show expressive language/behavioral/ organizational deficits	*Toddler:* functions normally on developmental/cognitive tests *Preschooler:* normal results for most; some show memory/perceptual/other cognitive deficits	small for height/weight; alert; talkative; friendly; exhibits fluttering movements; difficulty making transitions; severe tantrums; unable to handle wide range of stimuli; difficulty attending; motor/developmental delays; learning disabilities

Trying to get the cocaine-exposed infant to sleep may also be difficult. The infant may not be responsive to the usual parental methods for comforting. There may be prolonged periods of fussiness, and the child may seem to drop off to sleep only after exhausting himself. This, too, can be terribly discouraging for a new parent. Techniques for feeding and comforting are contained in Chapter Five.

OUTCOMES IN CHILDHOOD

During the toddler period (12 to 30 months), cocaine-exposed children tested lower on measures of development than nonexposed children. Nonetheless, their scores were within average range (9). Their play was seen as less age-appropriate and more impulsive, with shows of hitting and batting at different objects. This group of children was found to be less securely attached to parents and primary caregivers, which might be indicated by problems at separation and reunion times or difficulty adjusting to new environments. Language delays were noted in another study, as were a lack of tolerance for frustration and increased distractibility.

One researcher found that the majority of cocaine-exposed children tested by preschool age were within normal range on measures of development, language, and behavior (10). However, 30 percent to 40 percent of children studied showed varying degrees of problems with expressive language, attentional deficits, and behavioral organization. These results might well influence the length of time a child can participate in an activity, play with a toy, or stay involved in a conversation.

STRATEGIES FOR EARLY INTERVENTION

Many research results are preliminary, and further study is certainly indicated, but at this time special programs for cocaine-exposed infants and children seem unwarranted. There are clear indications, however, of the need for a series of other measures. Some form of intervention, such as home visits during the infant and toddler period, would be an appropriate preventative measure for children at risk. By having a health care, social work, or early childhood specialist regularly visit the family, the child's health and development could be continuously screened. At the same time parents could be learning about both development and behavior, and parenting competence could be increased.

When the need is indicated, the home visiting professional can make referrals to the appropriate agency or service. Such programs are already in place in some cities.

It is also essential that child care workers and primary school teachers receive training on the impact of addiction. This is the next group of adults likely to come into contact with the child. Information and training should include the effects of substance abuse on the child, the diversity of drug-affected families, and issues in the parent-child relationship. Educators must become aware of the ways that addiction impacts on family life—the effects on housing, income, nutrition, and lifestyle.

Opiates: The Known Effects

While heroin was once the drug of choice among illicit drug users, its use declined until the late 1950s and 1960s. At that time the resurgence created a corresponding interest in the prenatal and neonatal impacts of its use. Researchers have also looked into the effects of methadone exposure. Methadone is a prescription drug given to some persons recovering from heroin addiction, including pregnant women. Methadone allows a monitoring of and/or gradual withdrawal from drug use during pregnancy, rather than an abrupt one that might be hazardous to the fetus.

The most noted adverse effect of prenatal exposure to opiates is called *neonatal abstinence syndrome (NAS)*. The newborn experiences a series of withdrawal symptoms primarily affecting the digestive and central nervous systems. At the same time, many of the conditions present in the cocaine-exposed newborn, such as low birth weight and small head circumference, are also present in the opiate-exposed infant.

Most opiate-affected babies experience the onset of neonatal abstinence syndrome within 72 hours after birth (11). These can occur, however, in as few as 2, or as many as 14 days. The infant may show a decreased ability to pay attention to caretaking adults and to be responsive to social overtures.

As the symptoms of NAS become more pronounced, the infant is characterized by heightened sensitivity to many types of stimuli, including sound, light, and touch. The baby's digestive system may seem to function less effectively as feeding problems, loose stools, and frequent spitting up are observed. The baby that feeds poorly also becomes susceptible to dehydration and a loss of important electrolytes. What is at first mild tremoring can become more apparent as withdrawal progresses, and certain reflexes (especially rooting, sucking, and the startle response) may seem exaggerated. The infant may seem to constantly have a fist or hand in her or his mouth.

Another feature of neonatal abstinence syndrome is its effects on the respiratory system. The baby's nose may be constantly runny or stuffy. Breathing may seem rapid, and the chest may seem to contract as he takes in air. Some opiate-exposed infants exhibit poor color and experience apneaic episodes, when breathing stops altogether for short periods. For this reason, they may be at greater risk for Sudden Infant Death and may require an apnea monitoring system. Parents can learn to use this equipment in the home. Risk of SIDS is generally diminished by the end of the first year.

Most of the symptoms associated with neonatal abstinence syndrome disappear by two months of age; however, difficulty in comforting the baby may persist through the first year.

OUTCOMES IN CHILDHOOD

Research on prenatal opiate exposure began in earnest in the 1970s. To date, most studies suggest that children up to age 2 function within normal range on measures of developmental and cognitive abilities. The Bayley Mental Development Index and the Motor Development Index are two frequently used tests. While some studies indicated declines in cognitive and motor skills after one year, the research that included polydrug use, degree of prenatal care, and birth complications found fewer differences (12, 13).

When heroin-exposed children from 3 to 6 1/2 years were the subjects of a 1979 study, their language, cognitive functioning, and developmental abilities were tested (14). Although their play was found to be within normal range, the children functioned at a lower level than nonexposed children on tests of memory, perception, and other cognitive functions.

A study conducted in 1989 used the McCarthy Scale of Children's Abilities to evaluate 47 children at 4 1/2 years (15). No differences were found between exposed and nondrug-exposed groups of youngsters.

There are many difficulties encountered in studying the effects of drug exposure on children. Not the least of these is that mothers are less likely to stay involved in long-term research projects, and families may be transient and difficult to track. Further longitudinal studies are needed to clarify results to date. Research on the impact of parenting skills and home environment is also indicated. By the time a child enters the preschool years, the home setting has had opportunity to profoundly influence her development and potential. Some research shows that when maternal mental health, lifestyle, the effects of stress, and the stability of the child care arrangements are taken into account, no differences can be detected between opiate-affected and nonexposed children (16).

STRATEGIES FOR EARLY INTERVENTION

As for the cocaine-exposed child, special programs are contraindicated for the child who is prenatally opiate-exposed. Exceptions would occur when a diagnosed disability is present. There are, however, other forms of intervention that can be employed.

As a result of drug and alcohol abuse, referrals to child welfare systems have increased by as much as 300 percent in some communities (17). In Philadelphia, the increases are so substantial and the child welfare system so unprepared to deal with the onslaught, that referring agencies are told that parental drug abuse alone is insufficient reason for Department of Human Services' involvement.

Clearly, the psychosocial impact of parental drug abuse and the environment it creates must be made better known to state and federal legislators. Children endangered by familial addiction are the fastest growing population in the foster care system (18). In many cases, protective services for children may be the most efficient form of intervention, although it should be for the short term only. Without funds for social workers and the training and compensation of foster parents, such intervention is impossible.

Another much needed form of intervention must be support for parents through the community. Such systems of assistance could come to parents through churches, community groups, and even Narcotics Anonymous programs. While churches and community groups have already taken an interest in the prevention of child abuse, few have sufficient training or information to confront the problems associated with substance abuse.

Narcotics Anonymous, a self-help group that attempts to assist persons with recovery and relapse prevention, has not been substantially involved in parenting issues of the addicted. Parents could benefit from the support of others who share their experience, as well as from the input of trained facilitators. To offset the inevitable frustrations of parenting that can play a role in drug relapse and in child abuse and neglect, parents need to know that resources are available to them on a 24-hour basis. For many parents, it makes a tremendous difference to know that childrearing involves the same crises for almost everyone. In addition, information about the familial consequences of heroin addiction should be part of the preservice training for child care and other educators.

Alcohol: The Known Effects

Alcohol is seldom thought of as a drug. Its high rate of social acceptance across the world makes it a part of meals for many families, and its use is part of the rite of passage for entry into American adult life. Some children anticipate reaching legal drinking age as much as they look forward to the right to drive an automobile. Many children, however, have experimented with alcohol long before age 21, and its use has had a devastating impact on many families.

Among the licit and illicit drugs, alcohol is surely one of the most harmful. Both animal and human studies have long demonstrated that alcohol and its main metabolizing agent, acetaldehyde, are directly harmful to the developing fetus. At birth, the effects are obvious, and they are generally far-reaching.

Two terms are used in connection with prenatal alcohol exposure. *Fetal alcohol syndrome (FAS)* is defined as a group of birth defects, resulting from maternal alcohol abuse, that affect fetal growth and development of the brain and body. The term *fetal alcohol effects (FAE)* is used when there is only partial evidence of the effects of fetal alcohol syndrome. Why some children develop FAS and others only FAE is unknown. Rates of fetal alcohol syndrome range from one to three cases per 1,000 live births. Among Native Americans, who suffer from a higher instance of alcoholism, there are 9.8 cases per 1,000 births (19).

Alcohol affects the fetus by interfering with the transfer of crucial nutrients from mother to child. It also restricts the supply of oxygen to the fetus, and causes an excess production of prostoglandins that regulate cellular development and function. The result is a child with multiple impairments and malformations.

Low birth weight and intrauterine growth retardation affecting the body and head are common to alcohol-affected infants. The problems may only begin there. Malformations of the skull and facial features (craniofacial) may occur. These include: small eyes or short eye openings; malformation of the ears; a poorly defined philtrum (the vertical indentation between nose and mouth); a thin upper lip and nose; and flattened midfacial area. Crossed eyes (strabismus), heart murmurs, and liver or kidney problems are not uncommon problems.

As the newborn withdraws from the alcohol in his system he may exhibit heightened muscle tension, sleep problems, show reflex abnormalities, and be difficult to comfort. Fetal alcohol syndrome is also the leading known cause of mental retardation, although only about half of the children affected by FAS can be defined as retarded. In spite of what may seem to be obvious symptoms, the FAS or FAE diagnosis is often missed in infancy.

OUTCOMES IN CHILDHOOD

During the first two years of life, the characteristics of the newborn with fetal alcohol syndrome or fetal alcohol effects may persist. In addition to what has already been presented, the child may also be small for height and weight, be hyperexcitable, have difficulty adjusting to environmental stimuli, and have poor sleeping and eating behaviors.

While remaining small for chronological age, the preschooler with FAS/FAE may also appear to be alert, talkative, and friendly. She may exhibit fluttering arm and hand movements, and may find making transitions difficult. Her temper tantrums may be severe. Stimulation from a wide range of sources may alarm or upset her, and her attention span may be severely impaired. She may have motor and developmental delays or learning disabilities. Even when placed in a special program where she appears to be progressing, she may begin to manifest new problems.

STRATEGIES FOR EARLY INTERVENTION

A child with diagnosed fetal alcohol syndrome or fetal alcohol effects usually requires special education that may be lifelong. Specialists in dealing with FAS/FAE have recommended a series of strategies for early intervention with child and family (20). They suggest that the diagnosis of "failure to thrive" should invite specialists to investigate for fetal alcohol syndrome or fetal alcohol effects. The child's failure to grow and develop properly may indicate prenatal alcohol exposure. Early diagnosis is critical in order to begin providing the services needed and to avoid stigmatizing the child. Achieving early diagnosis goals may be dependent on additional training for professionals. They must become more familiar with symptoms, familial impact of addictions, and various forms of treatment (see Figure 4.3).

Both the professional and the parent are encouraged to see the behavioral problems associated with FAS/FAE in a different light. While temper tantrums, lying, and other forms of inappropriate behavior are not desirable in the child, seeing them in the light of the alcohol-exposed child's problems is beneficial. For a child who has poor impulse control, and who is seriously challenged by noise, light, or touch, these behaviors may be a way to escape what seems too difficult to handle.

Many suggestions are also made for working with parents. Parents with alcohol-related problems should be identified and referred for treatment whenever possible. Professionals should identify family strengths and build on them, rather than focusing on deficits. Parent support in the form of group meetings or individual counseling is considered helpful. Advice should be kept concrete and expectations realistic. Parents should be informed early if intervention for their child is expected to be lifelong.

Figure 4.3
Strategies for Early Intervention and Their Benefits

Home Visits

- To monitor child health
- To teach parenting skills, child development/behavioral information
- To refer children as needed for additional services

Child Care Worker/Teacher Training

- To provide information about the effects of substance abuse on child/family
- To provide information about the diversity of substance-affected families
- To develop skills for supporting the parent-child relationship

Full Funding of Child Welfare Agencies

- To provide ongoing parent support and education
- To provide funding for the foster care system and training of foster parents
- To prepare social workers to effectively deal with the effects of substance abuse on families

Use of Churches/Community and Narcotics Anonymous Groups

- To provide ongoing parent support and education
- To increase community awareness of the impact of substance abuse
- To destigmatize the substance-affected family

Early Diagnosis of Problems

- To avoid stigmatization of the child
- To identify parental and family problems that impact on the child
- To identify and build on family strengths

Tobacco Use, the Fetus, and the Child

It has been many years since the Surgeon General of the United Sates first warned smokers of the hazards of nicotine. In spite of media attention to the related health problems, the creation of many smoke-free work and recreational environments, and even lawsuits against tobacco manufacturers, smoking continues to be popular among many Americans. A growing body of research, however, indicates that in addition to the impact on the smoker herself, tobacco use has adverse effects on the developing fetus. As many as 7,000 infants die each year from health problems related to their mothers' smoking. Smoking may also cause up to 141,000 spontaneous abortions annually (21).

The addicting, psychoactive ingredient in cigarettes is nicotine. It acts on the user by both stimulating and relaxing her. It is also responsible for cancers and for respiratory and heart diseases. Nicotine affects the fetus by constricting the vessels that supply blood to the baby. The result can be early deatchment of the placenta from the wall of the uterus and/or rupture of the membranes that surround the fetus, leading to premature labor and delivery.

Some researchers suggest that maternal smoking contributes to the instance of congenital malformations—those problems caused by changes in certain genes. Hernias, heart defects, and cleft palate are all seen more frequently in the infants of women who smoke during pregnancy. Use of tobacco during pregnancy is known to cause reduced birthweight and smaller head and chest circumference in the newborn. These babies are also at increased risk of Sudden Infant Death during the first year. Researchers now believe that as many as 41 percent of SIDS cases are a result of parental smoking.

An additional complication of maternal tobacco use is the increase in upper respiratory illness in the infant and child. Asthma, bronchitis, pneumonia, and colds are more frequent in the children of smoking mothers. It is not yet known whether these problems originate with damage to fetal lungs, as some studies indicate, or if they result from passive exposure after birth.

As long as smoking is marketed as a sophisticated, adult activity, young women will continue to use tobacco and to endanger their babies.

Marijuana: Not a High for Babies

Marijuana is second only to alcohol as the most popular drug in America. Many people think of it as a harmless substance, and tout its medicinal uses for persons suffering the effects of glaucoma and chemotherapy.

The major psychoactive ingredient in marijuana is called delta-9-tetrahydrocannibinol or THC. It affects marijuana users by decreasing inhibitions and making them feel relaxed. Chronic users, however, can suffer from many of the same health problems as cigarette smokers, including bronchitis, emphysema, and asthma. Like nicotine, it constricts the blood vessels that supply oxygen to the fetus and increases levels of carbon monoxide in the mother's blood. Studies suggest that newborns exposed to high levels of marijuana in utero exhibit tremoring, heightened reflexes, and increased crying. In addition, the sleep and arousal states of the newborns are often affected. These symptoms usually disappear within 30 days after birth.

Although research on the effects of marijuana use has been going on for more than 150 years, information on the long-term impact of maternal use on the developing child is scarce. Some studies suggest that toddlers who have been prenatally exposed show diminished cognitive, language, and motor skills. Longitudinal research is clearly needed to determine exactly how the child is affected by this form of maternal drug use.

In Conclusion

In spite of a litany of problems faced by drug- and alcohol-exposed children, a broad range of interventions is possible; many of these can be quite effective. Education and health and human service professionals must be knowledgeable, realistic, and hopeful. Staying abreast of research and new treatment modalities through training, reading, meetings with colleagues, and conference attendance is critical to help make a future with potential for the child affected by substance abuse.

Endnotes

1. M.C. Rist. "The Shadow Children: Preparing for the Arrival of Crack Babies in School," *The American School Board Journal*, Research Bulletin, July, 1990, p. 1.

2. D.J. Besharov. American Enterprise Institute on Public Policy Research, Washington, DC, telephone interview, September 28, 1989.

3. Myers, B.J., O. Carmichael, and K. Kaltenbach. "Cocaine-Exposed Infants: Myths and Misunderstandings," *Zero to Three*, 13 (1), August/September, 1992, p. 1.

4. National Institute on Drug Abuse, Rockville, MD. *National Household Survey on Drug Abuse: Population Estimates 1990*. Washington, DC: U.S. Government Printing Office, 1991.

5. Zuckerman, B., et al. "Effects of Maternal Marijuana and Cocaine Use on Fetal Growth," *New England Journal of Medicine*, 320, 1989, pp. 762–768.

6. Zuckerman, B. "Drug-Exposed Infants: Understanding the Medical Risks," *The Future of Children*, 1 (1), 1991, pp. 22–35.

7. Ibid.

8. Kronstadt, D. "Complex Developmental Issues of Prenatal Drug Exposure," *The Future of Children*, 1 (1), 1991, pp. 36–49.

9. Chasnoff, I.J. "Cocaine: Two-year Follow-up of Infants," paper presented at the National Association for Perinatal Addiction Research and Education Conference, Miami, FL, December 1989.

10. Griffith, D.R. "Developmental Follow-up of Cocaine-exposed Infants to Three Years," paper presented at the International Society for Infant Studies, Montreal, 1990.

11. Finnegan, L.P., and K. Kaltenbach. "Neonatal Abstinence Syndrome." In Hockelman and Nelson (Eds.). *Primary Pediatric Care*. Second Edition. St. Louis, MO: Mosby Yearbook, Inc., 1992, pp. 1367–1378.

12. Chasnoff, I.J. "Maternal Non-Narcotic Substance Abuse During Pregnancy: Effects on Infant Development," *Journal of Neurobehavioral Toxicology and Teratology*, 6 (4), 1984, pp. 277–280.

13. Kaltenbach K., and L.P. Finnegan. "Developmental Outcome of Infants Exposed to Methadone in Utero: A Longitudinal Study, *Pediatric Research*, 9, 1987, pp. 311–313.

14. Wilson, G.S., et al. "The Development of Preschool Children of Heroin Addicted Mothers: A Controlled Study," *Pediatrics*, 63, 1979, pp. 135–141.

15. Kaltenbach K., and L.P. Finnegan. "Developmental Outcomes of Infants Exposed to Methadone in Utero: Assessment of Developmental and Cognitive Ability," *Prenatal Abuse of Licit and Illicit Drugs*. Vol. 562 of *Annals of the New York Academy of Sciences*, June 30, 1989, pp. 360–362.

16. Kaltenbach K., and L.P. Finnegan. "Developmental Outcomes of Children Born to Methadone-Maintained Women: A Review of Longitudinal Studies," *Journal of Neurobehavioral Toxicology and Teratology*, 6, 1984, pp. 271–275.

17. National Court-appointed Special Advocates Association, "Born into Addiction," *The Connection*, 5, Fall 1989, pp. 1–5.

18. McCullough, C.B. "The Child Welfare Response," *The Future of Children*, 1 (1), 1991, pp. 61–71.

19. Cook, P.S., R.C. Petersen, and D.T. Moore. *Alcohol, Tobacco and Other Drugs May Harm the Unborn*. Rockville, MD: U.S. Department of Health and Human Services, Office of Substance Abuse Prevention, 1990.

20. Olson, H.C., D.M. Burgess, and A. P. Streissguth. "Fetal Alcohol Syndrome (FAS) and Fetal Alcohol Effects (FAE): A Lifespan View with Implications for Early Intervention," *Zero to Three*, 13 (1), August/September, 1992, pp. 24–29.

21. As reported in *The Journal of Family Practice*, April 1995, pp. 385–394.

CHAPTER FIVE

Caring for Prenatally Drug-Exposed Children

Many types of programs, including foster care agencies, child care centers, family day care homes, church-sponsored nurseries, and group care facilities, have admitted drug-exposed infants and toddlers. Prenatal drug exposure alone should not be sufficient reason to exclude a child from a nonfamilial caregiving situation. In fact, appropriate group care and homelike settings that provide nonstressful and supportive childrearing are beneficial to the substance-exposed infant.

It is probably inadvisable, however, for infants to enter programs where adult caretakers have not been sufficiently prepared to work with them. Preparation should include learning about the specific effects of drug exposure; sensitization to family circumstances and needs; and skills for interacting with children and parents. Bias against and stigmatization of the substance-affected family can do great harm; damage resulting from unprofessional attitudes can hinder child development and mar the growth of the parent-child relationship.

Getting to Know Infant and Parent

First meetings of parent and infant with an education or human service worker should be low-key and relaxed. Professionals should be warm and approachable and, above all, willing to listen to parental concerns. Many adults with drug-abuse histories have reported a series of negative contacts with people in the "helping" professions. The parent may seem suspicious, or even hostile. It may be helpful to immediately raise the confidentiality issue. Parents may need to know that their private matters will not be discussed with other parents or agencies without written consent.

While talking with parents, the interviewer can observe parent-infant interactions. If the parent is comfortable with the arrangement, the baby can be placed in a nearby play area. This can provide the professional with an opportunity to converse with the adult, while perhaps providing initial insight into the degree to which the parent is alert to infant play and safety needs.

At the first meeting with parent and baby, information should be gathered about the infant's history. This chapter provides a sample questionnaire showing the types of questions that might be asked during an interview with a new parent (Figure 5.1). This is not a form that should be handed to the parent to complete. The questions are deliberately framed for use by an interviewer. Each parent's receptivity to and understanding of questions must be considered, and questions reframed to meet the needs of the individual.

Once questions have been answered, parents should be asked to regularly update program staff on any changes in family life or the baby's schedule. It can be explained that while infants and toddlers do not directly understand adult concerns, their behavior can be strongly affected by caregiver stress. Changes in infant feeding, sleeping, and elimination can be a direct result of family pressures.

Figure 5.1
Questionnaire for Parents/Primary Caregivers of
Prenatally Drug-Exposed Infants

___

Name of child: _____   Date of birth: _____

Nicknames: _____

Name of parent/guardian: _____

Address: _____   Telephone: _____

Mother's drug of choice: _____   Other drugs used : _____

Frequency of mother's present drug use: _____

Location of infant's birth: _____ Length of labor/delivery: _____

Infant's condition at birth: _____

Apgar score: _____ Length of hospitalization after birth: _____

Subsequent hospitalizations/dates : _____

Does infant have problems with any of the following? Check all that apply.

___ sleeping problems   ___ loose/flaccid muscles   ___ breathing difficulties

___ eating problems   ___ sensitivity to touch   ___ apneaic episodes

___ loose/watery stools   ___ constipation   ___ rapid breathing

___ frequent spitting up   ___ sensitivity to noise   ___ chest contractions

___ hypertonicity   ___ runny/stuffy nose   ___ seizures

___ crossed eyes   ___ sensitivity to light   ___ difficulty being comforted

Name of pediatrician: _____   Telephone: _____

Address: _____   Date of most recent examination: ____

Immunizations to date: _____

Medications currently prescribed by pediatrician: _____

_____

Conditions currently being treated for: _____

_____

Formula/types of foods infant presently eats: _____

_____

Infant's feeding schedule: _____

Infant's sleeping schedule: _____

Place infant sleeps: _____

Infant's elimination schedule: _____

Favorite toys/books: _____

Types of comforting infant is most responsive to: _____

_____

Favorite parent-child activities: _____

_____

Times with infant parent finds most difficult: _____

_____

Topics related to infant care/development parent would most like to learn about:

_____

Drug Exposure: Effects in the Early Months

As described in Chapter Four, there are a series of drug and alcohol impacts on prenatally exposed infants. While alcohol effects are more long term, those of illicit drugs may last for several weeks or months, as the drugs are slowly eliminated from the baby's system.

The infant may be slow to pick up weight or to grow in length. There may be eating difficulties. The baby may feed slowly and with evident discomfort, such as gas pain and frequent spitting up.

There is often a prolonged period of crying and inability to comfort the drug-exposed infant. This is rather like the colic that many mothers associate with healthy newborns during the first months of life; however, the intense crying and tenseness of the baby's body (a type of pronounced stretching behavior referred to as increased extensor tone or hypertonicity) can affect the success of techniques that would normally soothe the infant.

The exaggerated extensor tone makes it difficult for the infant to find a relaxed, comfortable position, and increases her or his level of stress. Feeding, sleeping, and times for adult-child interaction are negatively affected by these pronounced reflexive behaviors.

Techniques for Feeding

The substance-exposed baby may be unable to eat comfortably in a supine position, whether lying in a crib or being held by an adult. This position produces gas, abdominal pain, and frequent spitting up. A newly marketed infant feeding bottle can provide some relief, coupled with adjustments in the baby's position. The Healthflow® bottle is manufactured by the Johnson and Johnson Company, and is available in most stores that carry infant products. It is bent at an angle at the bottle's midpoint. This modification in design prevents air from being sucked into the baby's stomach, and can improve digestion. It is probably still advisable to put the baby into the crook of the arm in a semi-upright position (Figure 5.2). In addition, the baby should be allowed to feed for only short periods, followed by patting and burping sessions. In this way the caregiver can ascertain the infant's level of comfort and judge whether the feeding should continue. Some researchers suggest that parents should refrain from giving solid foods to drug-exposed infants for the first six months. This allows for a period of digestive system adjustment.

Parents and other caregivers should consider carefully the settings for infant feedings. Whenever possible, the drug-exposed baby should be held and fed in a quiet setting, away from other crying or playing children. The caregiver administering the bottle should be relaxed, as babies can sense adult tensions. Soft, soothing tones of voice should accompany the feeding process, and the caregiver should encourage the infant to eat without forcing her to eat more than she is physically comfortable accepting.

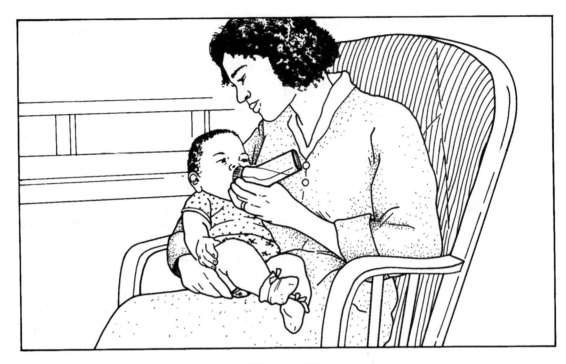

Figure 5.2

Infant may feed and interact most easily in semi-upright position.

BREASTFEEDING AND THE DRUG-EXPOSED INFANT

Although breastfeeding is widely advocated as providing the best food for babies, it may not be ideal for infants whose mothers continue to use drugs after delivery. Illicit and prescription drugs, alcohol, and nicotine ingested by a woman are secreted in her breast milk and can affect the health and behavior of the baby. Irritability, poor sleep patterns—even seizures and death—can result from the ingestion of various drugs through mother's milk.

Women are also discouraged from breastfeeding if they have used drugs intravenously or engaged in recent high-risk sexual activity. These may have exposed them to the human immunodeficiency virus (HIV) and to Acquired Immune Deficiency Syndrome (AIDS). Even if she has ceased having unprotected sex, it could be months before a test reveals the presence of disease. In the meantime, breastfeeding could expose the baby to the virus.

Discouraging breastfeeding among drug-addicted and recovering women can have disadvantages. They may feel less competent as mothers, and their self-image can be even more negatively affected. It can also be a deterrent to parent-child bonding. Although a physician or nurse may suggest bottle feeding, the woman may feel that it is the baby that is rejecting her.

Breastfeeding may be permissible if the mother is in a closely supervised treatment program, where she is regularly monitored for drug use. She should be highly motivated to nurse her infant, as most recovering persons have sufficient issues to confront without adding additional stressors. Even some methadone-maintained women can breastfeed for up to six months, if their drug dose is stable and carefully controlled. After six months, the growing infant ingests larger amounts of milk and may take in too much of the drug.

Holding and Comforting Techniques

Any parent who has ever had to cope with a screaming infant knows that the resulting frustration can test the mettle of the healthiest adult. Imagine for a moment, the impact of strenuous infant crying on an addicted or recovering parent. She tries rocking, singing to, even leaving the baby to "cry it out," to no avail. The child cries tirelessly, and the sound may be high-pitched and irritating. Even a dedicated professional caregiver can be sorely tested under these circumstances.

There may indeed be difficult periods for the baby prenatally exposed to drugs. If, however, the caregiver develops a grasp of how to work with and help the infant, these times need not be totally exasperating and the parent can also learn to work successfully with her child.

Every child is different; caregivers must study the individual baby to ascertain the types of stimuli that the child is comfortable with. Several years ago, writing about the psychosocial development of very young children, Stanley Greenspan cautioned that many of the infants described by parents as "difficult," simply gave off signals of need that parents had been unable to interpret. In a similar vein, T. Berry Brazelton and others confirm that infants give clear indications of their willingness to interact and the types of stimulation they can tolerate.

The tried-and-true technique of swaddling an infant is also comforting to drug-exposed babies. Swaddling means securely wrapping the child from neck to heels, or from chest to heels, in soft cloth. While this does restrict movement to a certain extent, it also inhibits tremoring or exaggerated reflexive behaviors that distress the infant. The youngest infants (neonates) may be most comforted by full-body swaddling, while older infants may enjoy having their hands free. Then they may reach for, grasp, and mouth interesting objects. If the baby is being held while swaddled, he or she can be held in a semiflexed or semi-upright position. This decreases exhibition of the extensor tone (Figure 5.3).

In many instances, rocking an infant is comforting when he or she is distressed. A good adult rocking chair or infant swing can be used; however, when using the swing, the young infant should be propped using rolled blankets on either side of the shoulders and head. They prevent the baby from flopping from side to side.

While some drug-exposed infants show an aversion to certain types of tactile stimulation, many enjoy immersion in a warm water bath. Using a small tub of water, place the baby in water heated to 99 to 101 degrees Fahrenheit (Figure 5.4). Note that this temperature is close to the body temperature of the infant. The baby should not be allowed to grow cold in the water, nor should she be left alone even momentarily. Her response to the water should be constantly monitored.

Figure 5.3

Swaddling reduces tremoring and exaggerated extensor tone

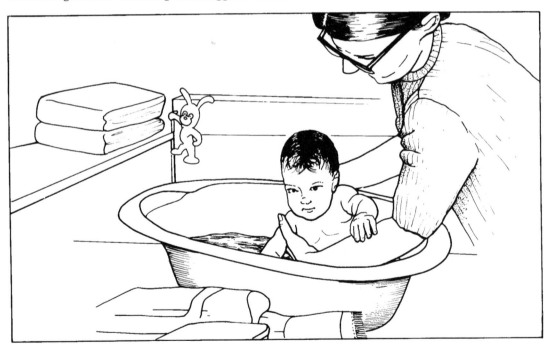

Figure 5.4

Immersion in a warm bath can be comforting

Among those who have worked with drug-exposed infants, there is disagreement about some forms of handling. Several sources recommend only the gentlest of pats and rubs of the baby's body. The authors found, however, that some infants responded only to firm patting as an effective soothing technique. These children enjoyed being stretched across the adult's knees and having their backs rubbed or patted with a firm, but not hard, stroke (Figure 5.5).

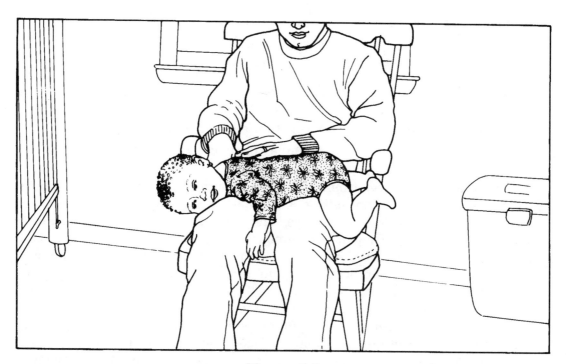

Figure 5.5

Patting or rubbing the infant's back can be comforting

A child who is ready to interact makes eye contact and moves his mouth to make cooing or gurgling sounds. His body movements may be slow and rhythmic or excited, but they indicate his pleasure at adult attentions (Figure 5.6).

Figure 5.6
Infant Communications

Signs of Pleasure: *Willingness to Interact*	*Signs of Distress:* *Overstimulation*
• making eye contact • cooing or gurgling • rhythmic movement • playful wiggling • smiling • relaxed posture	• averting eyes • grimacing or frowning • frequent yawning • hiccuping • spitting up • constant sucking of hands/fingers • change in color (to pale, red, or bluish)

An infant who is overstimulated, tired or hungry, averts his gaze, yawns, hiccups, spits up, and eventually cries. Babies who cannot handle their surroundings may also frown or grimace. They may stare at their hands, rather than at nearby adults. They may strenuously suck on their fingers or hands. If an arm or leg is stroked, the baby may retract it. Under real duress, the baby may literally change color, becoming pale, red, or even bluish. In these ways, infants attempt to relieve the stress they feel and to comfort themselves. Each of these behaviors represents a clear message to "stop it."

Among babies in general, some do not enjoy tactile stimulation. Heavy or rough blankets or clothing and cold surfaces may distress the infant. These babies do not appreciate prolonged episodes of cuddling, kissing, or hugging. Caregivers and parents must learn to read these forms of infant communication, and to appreciate that they also signal the uniqueness of the individual child.

Caregivers will discover that some drug-exposed babies do not like being held in positions where they are forced to make eye contact with others (Figure 5.7). The pressure to make eye contact may be too much for these infants, so they will avert their eyes and turn their heads away. Parents will need to know that this is not a rejection of them, merely a coping mechanism that the child temporarily employs. The baby could also be responding to abdominal discomfort that many drug-exposed infants experience. In this instance, elevating the baby to a semi-upright position in the crook of the adult's arm can be helpful. Some children prefer to be positioned on the caregiver's shoulder, where face-to-face contact is less frequent and the world can be taken in from a distance.

Figure 5.7
Holding and Comforting Techniques for Drug-exposed Infants

- Hold baby in semi-upright position.
- Hold baby facing away from adult's body.
- Swaddle the baby from neck or chest down.
- Rock baby in rocking chair or infant swing.
- Place baby in warm bath of 99 to 101 degrees.
- Pat or rub baby's back.
- Massage baby's trunk or limbs.
- Place baby in front carry pack for outings.

Carrying positions can also have a bearing on the infant's level of comfort. In working with a range of babies that had experienced prenatal drug exposure, we found that carrying the infant on the hip facing away from the body, with the arm across the abdomen and the thighs supported by the caregiver's other arm seems to relieve discomfort (Figure 5.8). At the same time, the child can observe the world from a less stressful distance.

Figure 5.8

Carrying position on hip with thighs supported

Many babies enjoy a gentle massage of their limbs or trunk (Figure 5.9). Caregivers should heed the responses of the individual infant as to which part of the body can accept touches. If the child is too sensitive to stimulation of a certain area, she or he will often retract that area or flinch at the touch. Use of baby lotion or a small amount of oil can help the infant feel more relaxed, and makes movement of the adult's hands over the body more soothing. There are several good references available for learning infant massage techniques.

When taking a young baby on an outing, a front carry infant pack is recommended, rather than a stroller or coach. Unless the baby is extremely sensitive to tactile stimuli, the sound of the adult's beating heart and body warmth are usually comforting. It is also advisable to remember that trips to stores and malls are more enjoyable to adults than to young children. Even a healthy newborn usually falls asleep under these circumstances. Sleeping is the baby's way of coping with overstimulation. For drug-exposed infants, outings should be kept short, and adults should remain alert to indications of stress.

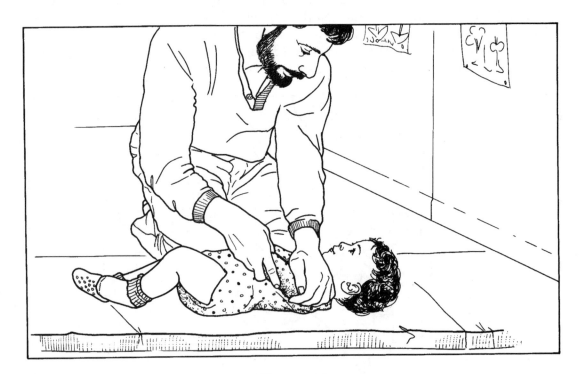

Figure 5.9

Infant massage techniques can relax and soothe some babies

Positions for Play and Exploration

One goal for early intervention with drug-exposed infants is helping the child to develop sustained interest in and tolerance for her environment. An additional aim is to help the baby develop control over her reflexes and responses to stimuli. Work toward these ends, in part, by positioning the infant in ways that permit her to visually and tactilely explore the environment. It is important that the baby be able to do these things at her own pace, without constant facilitation by adults.

One play position for young infants is the prone position, where the child is placed on his stomach (Figure 5.10). Although he will still exhibit extensor tone, it will be the type where he pushes against the force of gravity, rather than stretching with it. Interesting toys should be placed within visual and grasping range. This position also develops upper body and neck muscle strength.

Figure 5.10

On his stomach the infant can explore his surroundings and develop motor skills

If the baby is placed on her back, she can be helped to overcome exaggerated extensor tone by placing a cushion under her hips to elevate the pelvis. The knees are then directed back toward the chest and the infant engages in desired kicking and foot play activities. Rolled cloth or blankets under the shoulders help to bring the baby's hands to midline (center of the chest). This promotes hand play and examination of objects (Figure 5.11). Babies should not be left on their backs to nap or sleep.

Figure 5.11

For comfort on her back, the infant's pelvis and shoulders must be properly supported

Infants can also be placed on their sides, if properly supported by rolled blankets at the back and between the legs (Figure 5.12). There is even a new device available for parents to keep babies in the side position. If the legs are not also properly supported, however, the drug-affected baby will arch backward into a hypertonic position.

In the semiflexed position afforded by an infant seat, the young baby can easily survey his world. Once again, he may require rolled blankets under the shoulders to keep from slipping from side to side. The blankets also keep the hands at midline (Figure 5.13).

If a baby is seated with adult support, the surface should be firm and the infant should be bent slightly forward at the hips (Figure 5.14). This prevents the child from rearing backward because of exaggerated extensor tone.

Drug-exposed babies truly enjoy standing with caregiver support. Both this position and the use of walkers should be strongly discouraged, as they may promote hypertonicity. Most pediatricians and safety experts are warning parents that walkers are unsafe under any circumstances. More than 20,000 accidents occur annually as a result of walker use.

While trying various positions, caregivers and parents are advised to watch for the reactions of the individual infant. What makes one baby feel comfortable and relaxed can be stressful for another. As babies grow and develop new positions can be tried.

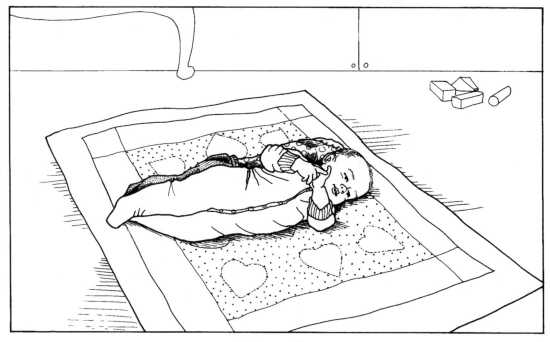

Figure 5.12

In the side position, support the infant's back and legs

Figure 5.13

Provide shoulder support while using an infant seat

Figure 5.14

Tilt the seated infant forward at the hips

Issues for New Mothers

The outstanding feature of childbirth under most circumstances is that it is a joyous and welcomed event. This is not necessarily the case with mothers who abuse drugs. The baby may present another in a series of life complications that she is not prepared to handle. On the other hand, if she welcomes the birth, it may not be for the best of reasons. A pregnancy and new baby bring attention and emotional support that may be otherwise lacking in the woman's life. Newborns bring praise for a job well done, and gifts. For a mother with a poor sense of self-worth and a hunger for positive feedback, a new baby may provide a much-needed emotional high.

Addiction and recovery from addiction carry with them a unique set of problems for the new mother. The woman may be extremely egocentric, and when the focus is primarily on her own needs, she may be unable or unwilling to address those of her baby. It may be easier for her to push the care of her infant on others, if the baby is not neglected altogether.

Yet another type of mother lavishes care on her baby in a compulsive fashion. She feels unable to be apart from him, even for short periods. She buys inappropriate amounts of toys and clothing for him, yet may neglect her own health and appearance.

Most addicted persons are, at some level, aware that their drug use poses a problem for them. This is true even when an individual seems to be in denial. There may be a defensive veneer developed to ward off attacks related to their substance abuse. Even early in recovery, they may insist that the impact of their drug use on their family members has been minimal. When professionals approach to provide parenting information, they are rebuffed. A mother may steadfastly argue that she does not need assistance, even when parenting is clearly stressful for her. Persistence by professionals may be met with hostility and anger.

It is important to recognize that underlying these rejections is a tremendous fear of criticism. If the parent acknowledges her lack of competence, she admits yet another failure in a life fraught with failures, so it is easier to deny that a problem exists.

Denial is one way that the drug-addicted mother copes. Many substance abusers learn to deny parental addiction and family dysfunction in childhood. As they grow to adulthood, the denial continues. Their substance abuse must be hidden from others. So while the parent may desperately need parenting help, she is not apt to ask for it.

Another series of problems for addicted parents is related to public perceptions of their drug use. These mothers and fathers have not missed the "crack baby" reports in the media. They are sensitive to hostilities toward substance-abusing parents, and the view that maternal drug use constitutes deliberate abuse of the fetus. Most parents worry about whether their behavior has influenced their baby's health; however, they may not be able to differentiate between the postnatal effects of past drug use, and the ongoing impact of their lifestyle on the child. When the professional urges the parent to develop a schedule for the baby, to try different feeding techniques, or to attempt different modes of interaction, these suggestions often imply that something is wrong with the baby. If something is wrong with the infant, the *blame* then rests with the mother.

Roles for Professionals

The very last thing that the substance-abusing or recovering mother needs to feel is more guilt. Professionals must become adept at identifying family strengths and helping parents to see these themselves. Each small effort to be a good caretaker of her newborn should be recognized and praised. The parent should be asked, rather than told, what she would like to learn about childrearing. It should be acceptable if she initially says that she does not need any information. Only after the parent's confidence has been raised and a trusting relationship built can the professional hope to successfully address problems.

It can be difficult for the professional to accept that an enormous investment of time and energy must occur in order for a small change to be perceived. Parents must often work for a long time on their own issues before they can begin to tackle those related to parenting. Substance-abusing adults know that they are not perfect, and they want to be good parents. To achieve this end, time and patience are required. Professionals must lend their expertise and support. We must think of ourselves as builders of strong families, who can ultimately provide adequate care and nurturance for their children.

Resources

American Academy of Pediatrics Committee on Drugs. "Transfer of Drugs and Other Chemicals into Human Milk," *Pediatrics*, 84, 1989, pp. 924–936.

Auckett, A. *Baby Massage: Parent-Child Bonding Through Touch*. New York: Newmarket Press, 1988.

Bassett, M. *Infant and Child Care Skills*. New York: Delmar Publishers, 1995.

Brazelton, T.B. *On Becoming a Family*. New York: Delacorte Press, 1992.

Brazelton, T.B. *Touchpoints: Your Child's Emotional and Behavioral Development*. Boston: Addison-Wesley, 1992.

Brown, C.C. (Ed.). *Infants at Risk*. Chicago, IL: Johnson and Johnson, 1981.

Caldwell Brown, C. *Childhood Learning Disabilities and Prenatal Risk*. Chicago, IL: Johnson and Johnson, 1983.

Caldwell Brown, C. *The Many Facets of Touch*. Chicago, IL: Johnson and Johnson, 1984.

Castle, K. *The Infant and Toddler Handbook*. Atlanta, GA: Humanics, Ltd., 1990.

Dixon, S., K. Breshnahan, and B. Zuckerman. "Cocaine Babies: Meeting the Challenge of Management," *Contemporary Pediatrics*. 7, 1990, pp. 70–92.

Forrest, D.C., "The Cocaine-exposed Infant, Part II: Intervention and Teaching," *Journal of Pediatric Health Care*. 8, 1994, pp. 7–11.

Gonzalez-Mena, J., and D.W. Eyer. *Infants, Toddlers and Caregivers*. Third Edition. Mountain View, CA: Mayfield Publishing Company, 1993.

Greenspan, S. *First Feelings*. New York: Viking Press, 1989.

Gunzenhauser, N. *Advances in Touch*. Chicago, IL: Johnson and Johnson, 1991.

Gunzenhauser, N. *Infant Stimulation*. Chicago, IL: Johnson and Johnson, 1991.

Hansen, B., and L. Moore. "Recreational Drug Use by the Breastfeeding Woman: Part I: Illicit Drugs," *Journal of Human Lactation*. 5 (4), 1989, pp. 178–180.

Howard, J., et al, "The Development of Young Children of Substance-abusing Parents: Insights from Seven Years of Intervention and Research," *Zero to Three*. 9, 1989, pp. 8–12.

Klaus, M.H. (Ed.). *Maternal Attachment and Mothering Disorders*. Chicago, IL: Johnson and Johnson, 1978.

Lucas, K., B. Bennett, and N. Schneider. "The Case of Infants Menaced by Cocaine Abuse," *Maternal Child Nursing*. 14, 1989, pp. 324–329.

Lynch, M., and V. McKeon. "Cocaine Abuse During Pregnancy," *Journal of Gynecological and Neonatal Nursing*. 19, 1990, pp. 285–292.

Miller, K. *Things to Do with Toddlers and Twos*. Marshfield, MA: Telshare Publishing Company, Inc., 1984.

Sasserath, V. (Ed.). *Minimizing High-risk Parenting*. Chicago, IL: Johnson and Johnson, 1983.

Schneider, J., D. Griffith, and I. Chasnoff. "Infants Exposed to Cocaine in Utero: Implications for Developmental Assessment and Intervention," *Infants and Young Children*. 2, 1989, pp. 25–36.

Silverman, N. *Recommendations for Breastfeeding in Drug-dependent Women*. Philadelphia, PA: Thomas Jefferson University, April 1994.

Stonehouse, A. *Trusting Toddlers: Planning for One-to-Three Year Olds in Child Care Centers*. St. Paul, MN: Redleaf Press.

Thomas, E.B., and S. Trotter (Eds.). *The Social Responsiveness of Infants*. Chicago, IL: Johnson and Johnson, 1978.

Weston, D., B. Ivins and D. Zuckerman. "Drug-exposed Babies: Research and Clinical Issues," *Zero to Three*. 9, 1989, pp. 1–7.

Wilson. L.C., L. Watson and M.A. Watson. *Infants and Toddlers: Curriculum and Teaching*. New York: Delmar Publishers, Inc., 1995.

CHAPTER SIX

Developing Programs for Substance-Affected Children

A child's exposure to drugs and alcohol does not have to be direct. As devastating as maternal use during pregnancy can be for the fetus, it can be equally traumatic for a parent to develop an addiction while parenting. Even the ups and downs of the drug or alcohol recovery process can severely complicate a child's life. Early childhood educators and others working with drug- and alcohol-affected children must comprehend the impact of substance abuse on the child's life and development in order to plan effective programs.

Problems of Children of Addicted Parents

There are many ways a child can be affected by familial addiction. The degree of impact is often dependent upon the child's stage of development, individual personality, needs, and coping skills. For example, a toddler, typically characterized by intense willfulness and egocentrism, has a strong need for a dependable, stable adult in her life. The usually gregarious and loquacious preschooler needs an interested and patient adult in his life. As the school-age child embarks on new experiences with friendships and school, she needs support and understanding. The teenager looks to his adults for modeling and gradual increases in privilege and responsibility. During any one of these stages, or as a thread throughout them all, parental addiction is a major threat to a child's healthy development.

Drug use affects the individual's awareness of others. The needs of a young dependent child may be sidelined by the parent's need to use drugs or alcohol. The child of an addict may not have the most basic of needs addressed. Clean clothing, regular meals, even diaper changes may be neglected. Needs for comforting and holding may be ignored. As addiction progresses, the addicted person's entire life is governed by the need to "get high." The child may be seen as a barrier to that goal. His life is dictated by the parent's own erratic and unpredictable behavior and lifestyle.

Especially during the early childhood years, the child needs attentive reinforcement for healthy development to occur. Milestones must be recognized and applauded as they occur. For the child of an addicted parent, this support may not be forthcoming. The child may speak, but receive no response; may speak and be told to "shut up." The parent may regularly be impatient or angry with the child, at other times disinterested or apathetic. These responses do little for the child's self-esteem or security needs.

Human beings, both adults and children, need a sense of control over their world. This means developing a sense that in some slight way one can impact in positive ways on his or her life. The child of the addicted parent does not develop this essential *internal locus of control*. Instead, the out-of-control parent creates a world for the child that is entirely unreliable and uncertain.

An Absence of Social and Language Skills

Growing up in a substance-affected environment plays havoc with a young child's social and language skills development. The drug-abusing parent tends to isolate herself from nonusing family and community. In this way, she is protected from exposure and criticism about her parenting abilities. Closeted with others who abuse drugs and alcohol, she also restricts the social contacts of her children, and several types of effects are possible.

First, the child may learn at an early age to be secretive about his parent's activities. He may be cautioned repeatedly not to discuss family business, and may be prohibited from bringing playmates to the family home. She may grow to accept this secretiveness and the associated anxiety as a normal part of life. Her sense of trust in others can become permanently impaired.

It should be noted that in some cases parents successfully hide an addiction from their children. The children know that something is seriously wrong, but are unaware of the cause. These children, on discovering the truth, may experience a profound sense of betrayal and disappointment.

Children may be socially affected in yet another way. No matter how hard an addict may try to hide her problems from others, family and neighbors usually see the telltale signs. Changes in the addict's behavior and friendships, appearance, and lifestyle are among the symptoms of substance abuse. The children are drawn into the lifestyle and are neglected in the same ways that the parent neglects himself or herself. The child picks up inappropriate language, gestures, and drug jargon, and invariably becomes as unacceptable to the nonusing community as the parent. Lacking in social know-how, the child is ostracized by adults and other children.

In this chapter, we explore the ways in which the child development program, early childhood education classroom, or playroom can be the arena in which essential language and behavioral skills can be learned.

Planning a Program for Substance-Affected Children

There is a critical need for programs and practices to support children who have been prenatally or environmentally exposed to drugs and alcohol. Special settings and equipment are generally unnecessary. Rather, careful planning of curriculum and environment, and thoughtful selection of staff are the keys to a successful program. Furthermore, segregation of substance-affected children in "crack baby classrooms" is not an effective solution to this problem, any more than it was desirable to isolate children with disabilities. Children whose parents abuse drugs and alcohol, except in the instance of those profoundly affected by fetal alcohol syndrome, need a mainstream environment in which they can begin preparing for life and schooling outside of the community of substance-abusing individuals.

DEVELOPING PROGRAM GOALS

Whether developing a Parent-Child Center as a feature of drug and alcohol treatment, or attempting to mainstream affected children into an existing classroom or program, the identification of goals is essential. It is the goals or primary aims that set forth a clear-cut agenda for the program. The effects of prenatal or environmental substance abuse on children provide suggestions for specific goals (Figure 6.1). For example:

1. The program should support the growth of the parent-child relationship. While any high quality children's program should have such a purpose, supporting parent-child attachment and interactions within the context of the drug-affected family is crucial. Drug-abusing parents tend to have experienced a greater degree of family dysfunction in their own upbringing, and may have difficulty perceiving the rewards of child rearing in adult life. Parental substance abuse is known to interfere with the normal evolution of attachment relations, and may increase the likelihood of child abuse and neglect. The parent may lack knowledge of the qualities of an "effective" parent.

Support for the parent-child relationship comes in the form of activities to model appropriate parenting behaviors; to raise parental self-esteem; and to reinforce the growth of parental competence.

2. The program should support the developing self-esteem of both parent and child. Early childhood educators have long recognized the importance of helping children to develop self-awareness and positive feelings about self. In most cases, the child's self-image is strongly linked to that of his or her parent. When one's self-esteem is raised, so is the other's. In drug-affected families, negative self-images arise as parents and children compare their own with other families. Self-esteem is further lowered by feelings of guilt and inadequacy.

Self-esteem building is a slow, time-taking process based on recognition of the uniqueness of the individual parent and child. Activities must be offered to promote and assure some successes, while helping the person to accept and cope with occasional failure (see Chapter Seven for examples).

3. The program should assist the child in the development of positive and acceptable social behaviors. The substance-abusing family does not always offer its children guidance and feedback on behavior. Rules and consistent consequences for misbehavior may be nonexistent. Even when rules are offered, they may not match the child's developmental level, and expectations may be too high, or too low.

The program must acknowledge the strengths of each child and build on these, adopting a positive model rather than a deficit approach. Consistently applied rules and reliable adults are two ingredients for helping children build the essential social skills.

4. The program should support the growth of the child's developmentally and socially appropriate language skills. To function successfully in school and adult life settings, a child must develop listening and verbal skills. When substance abuse intervenes in family life, the child may lack key communications abilities. He or she may develop inappropriate language and corresponding behaviors instead.

Program staff can provide both language modeling and feedback for the child. In interactions with parents, this modeling can be extended to begin to affect the language of the child's home life. Conversation, games, books, and stories are among the activities to benefit both adult and child.

5. *The program should provide an environment to promote the child's sense of security and belongingness.* Substance exposure results in the isolation of affected children. Social and emotional isolation results from parental drug and alcohol abuse, causing the child to wonder where and with whom he belongs. Erratic behavior of parents interferes with the safety and security needs of the child, and antisocial feelings of mistrust can evolve.

The program can assist the child in these areas by creating a child-friendly environment. This setting facilitates the child's sense of ownership of the space and recognition of others as co-owners, and promotes membership in the classroom "family."

6. *The program must assure that children are properly screened for the health problems and developmental delays that can accompany upbringing in a drug-affected environment.* Whether the result of parental neglect or ignorance, the child's poor health or failure to develop according to norms may influence academic success and future growth.

Linkages should be promoted with screening programs and specialists in order to identify problems or delays while the child is young and intervention is most likely to be effective.

Figure 6.1
Goals for Programs Serving Substance-Affected Children

---

1. To support the growth of the parent-child relationship.
2. To support the developing self-esteem of both parent and child.
3. To assist the child in the development of positive, acceptable modes of social behavior.
4. To support the growth of the child's socially and developmentally appropriate language skills.
5. To provide an environment to promote the child's sense of security and belonging.
6. To undertake health and developmental screenings designed to assure that each child has opportunities to reach full potential.

STAFFING PROGRAMS

Even when physical environments, equipment, and materials are not ideal, high quality programming can be achieved with knowledgeable, dedicated staff.

Much has been written about the characteristics of "good" early childhood educators. Knowledge of child development, patience, and a sincere interest in children are among those touted as essential skills. When selecting staff to serve substance-affected children and their parents an entirely new set of abilities comes into focus.

These individuals should be *free of prejudices, especially those related to drug and alcohol abuse*. While few people are innately bias free, those who have the quality of open-mindedness can learn via training and experience to let go of previous misconceptions that might interfere with work with families (Figure 6.2).

Empathy, not pity, is another desirable trait for those working with substance-exposed children. While one should be able to *feel compassion and concern*, the ability to *balance and handle emotions appropriately* is also necessary. One would not benefit families by feeling that he or she could do a much better job of parenting the children, nor is it healthy for educators and health or human service providers to care so deeply for individual children as to desire to replace the child's parents. The ability to keep ones self in balance gives perspective and prevents overload and burnout in caring and dedicated staff.

Yet another important quality is *insight into one's own strengths and weaknesses*. Persons working with families affected by substance abuse must accept the notion that it may be only accidents of birth, upbringing, or temperament that separate the workers from the clients. Few of us have been sufficiently tested to know what our reaction would be to some of the life circumstances faced by drug-affected families.

Finally, staff members should have the *capacity for fair and judicious use of power*. Some adults, lacking control in their own lives, enjoy wielding power over others. A successful program is one that begins the process of empowering children to take control of their lives via adults who *facilitate* rather than *dictate*.

Ideas for staff training are suggested by many of the topics in this volume. The extent of the drug and alcohol abuse problem, the various types of drugs used and their effects, types of treatment available, characteristics of abusers, and prenatal effects of substance abuse are only a few of the subjects for the education of effective and knowledgeable staff.

Creating Environments for Substance-Affected Children

The environment of any classroom or playroom has three basic elements: atmosphere, layout, and materials/equipment. Each of these aspects plays a different but contributory role in making an effective environment. In this section, we will examine each of these elements and the characteristics that contribute to a quality program for children from birth up to age 8.

THE ATMOSPHERE

Classroom atmosphere is made up of both physical aspects of space and the human interaction that occurs within it (Figure 6.3). The physical component consists of comfort levels created by color use, lighting, and temperature. A positive atmosphere is indicated by the ways that people using the space communicate and interface with one another.

It may seem to an adult that an environment is physically comfortable; however, adults do not always take into account the differences between their own and the child's level of comfort. A child who moves around a space busily may be more comfortable with a lower room temperature than an adult moving at a slower, more purposeful rate; however, a child may also lack weather or climate-appropriate clothing, and the thermostat may need adjustment to reflect the child's dress.

Children from substance-abusing environments may have their health care neglected. The problem may arise from parental ignorance of child health issues; from financial need; from impoverished environments; or even from the inability to face a child's potential problems. The children may suffer from higher instances of colds, bouts of influenza, ear infections, iron deficiency anemia, and undiagnosed special needs. Each of these health problems may require an adjustment of the classroom environment. Regular changing of the air in the classroom, frequent washing of toys and other items handled by children, and the posting of essential health information are some ways of helping the environment to reflect children's needs.

Among child developmentalists and early childhood educators there is a heartfelt belief that children are children, regardless of ethnic background, religion, socioeconomic group, or physical or mental condition. Therefore, they should be treated with respect, listened to, and responded to with concern and consistency. The substance-exposed child is no different from any other child, except that she may have lacked these types of responses from the adults in her life. Adults working in the classroom should remember that even the youngest child looks to them for support and models of positive styles of interaction.

LAYOUT

Layout refers to the arrangement of materials and equipment within the allotted space. The layout of a classroom or playroom for young children should involve a series of considerations; many of these are consistent with any high-quality educational or developmental program.

Unless a space is designed specifically for use by children, the adults who determine the layout must take into account the size and resources afforded by the room. Natural alcoves, sources of water, and window lighting are some examples of natural resources that might be utilized as a classroom is set up. An area for art can be placed near a water supply; a sunny window invites a book area.

The layout should show attention to the developmental levels of the children who will use it. Sufficient space should be provided for the various types of

Figure 6.2
Characteristics of Staff Working with Substance-Affected Children

- Free of prejudices related to drug and alcohol abuse
- Open-minded
- Empathic
- Able to balance and handle emotions appropriately
- Has insight into own strengths and weaknesses
- Uses power fairly and judiciously

Figure 6.3
Creating Environments for Children

Atmosphere

- low-key room color
- sufficient lighting to provide for various types of activity
- comfortable temperature with attention to children's activity levels, clothing, and health condition
- verbal respect for the child and his or her possessions
- adults who are attentive to children's communications
- consistent adult responses to children and their behavior

Layout

- shows attention to developmental levels of children
- shows attention to children's interests
- displays uncluttered and at children's eye level
- has clearly defined interest centers
- is visually attractive, appealing to children
- shows use of room parameters and natural resources

Equipment / Materials

- are child-sized
- can be easily washed or cleaned
- can stand up under normal or rough child's play
- are safe for the age of child receiving services
- provide a range of learning experiences
- are available in sufficient quantities to enable play by several children simultaneously

activities that young children engage in: active and quiet, small motor and large motor, group and individual. Equipment and materials should be displayed at the children's eye level, and their arrangement should be attractive and uncluttered. Beginning around age 2, children can be responsive to the pictorial labeling of areas and materials. In this way, adults help children to respect equipment and to understand the proper uses of the various centers in the room.

Areas designated for specific types of play are commonly referred to as *interest centers*. Typical interest centers found in the early childhood classroom are: Housekeeping, Library, Blocks, Sand/Water, Table Toys, Music, and Art (Figure 6.4). The issue is not, however, how many of these areas are included, but rather that those selected be of *value* and *interest* to the children.

Value to children may be equated with the learning of new skills and concepts, or with cathartic activity. For children who have experienced severe anxiety or trauma, the Housekeeping Area may invite acting out of worrisome home experiences. Children may also have the opportunity to practice nurturing behaviors. The Block Area may provide a place to release tension and learn appropriate social skills while engaging in large muscle play. Interest to children is determined by their age and developmental levels. Interest can also be affected by popular television shows or movies, books, or stories.

A properly arranged and equipped classroom can serve several age groups. Interest centers should be clearly defined through the use of dividers, area rugs, and strategically placed furniture. Children should regard their classroom as a reliable space that invites their play and exploration. It should be a space whose layout provides guidance as to how to behave in it.

MATERIALS AND EQUIPMENT

Classroom supplies, or equipment and materials, should meet a set of basic standards in order to most benefit the children who will use them. They should be sized to the height or hand size of the children. They should be washable or easily cleanable in order to help maintain a healthy environment. They should be safe for use by young children, and durable—standing up under daily rough-and-tumble use.

When purchasing equipment and materials, the numbers of children in the group should be considered. For children entering the program with few social skills, being asked to wait for a turn with a favorite toy may be difficult. There should be sufficient numbers of items so that several children can play at one time.

Children should be provided with materials and equipment that offer a range of learning experiences. A toy with only one purpose is generally a waste of valuable funds. Items that can be enjoyed in more than one interest center, teach several types of skills, and afford opportunities for creativity offer children the best learning experiences.

Figure 6.4
Basic Interest Centers, Materials, and Equipment

Housekeeping Area

- child-sized appliances (stove, sink, refrigerator)
- table and chairs
- toy dishes, eating utensils
- toy telephone
- dolls, doll bed or coach
- dress-up clothes

Block Area

- unit blocks or other construction toys
- toy cars and trucks
- family or community helper figures
- miniature traffic signs

Table Toys

- small building blocks
- puzzles
- lotto games
- stringing beads
- pegs and pegboard

Art Area

- tempera paints (red, blue, yellow)
- paintbrushes
- art paper
- glue or paste

Library Area

- age-appropriate books
- book display shelf
- colorful wall posters
- cushions or chairs
- cassette player
- story audiotapes
- flannel board

Sand / Water Play Area

- sand/water table or large containers
- scoops or shovels
- sieves or strainers
- molds or cookie cutters

Music Area

- child-sized instruments
- record or cassette player
- records or cassettes —blank and with variety of music
- scarves

- scissors
- large crayons and markers
- play dough

Curriculum and Scheduling Issues

Among some parents and teachers there is a belief that educating young children involves teaching academic skills at an earlier age. They believe that the young child should be learning to read, write, and solve math problems. This understanding of education for children under 5 is the antithesis of the philosophy of most early childhood educators. Our concern is that children develop a solid foundation of physical, cognitive, language, and social experiences upon which to build the later more complex skills and concepts.

In the case of the substance-affected child, the need for foundation building may be critical, as experiences normally provided by parents may be lacking. The child may enter a program without even simple experiences with naming objects, learning colors, or hearing stories or childhood rhymes. The adults working with this child should assume nothing. A wait-and-watch attitude should be adopted in order to take the time to assess the child's levels of knowledge and skills. New experiences can then be based upon the outcomes of these observations.

Providing time for children to learn the rules of the classroom is as much a curricular issue as the planning of an art or music activity. The child needs time to become familiar with a new environment that makes a specific set of demands on him. He will need many chances to learn the rules and to test the adults that created them. It behooves adults working with young children to remember this rule:

> The teaching of social and behavioral skills should be handled no differently from the teaching of colors or shapes. If a child does not know his colors, we patiently name them and give many chances for him to learn them. So should we patiently give him chances to learn to share, cooperate, and to take turns.

In the beginning of this chapter we suggested that programs for substance-affected children should provide them with opportunities to develop a sense of control over their world, as well as feelings of security and belonging. It is for these reasons that we suggest that those administering programs consider suspending the need for an incessant string of planned activities. In reality, a tight schedule meets adult rather than child needs.

We are not suggesting a lack of planning, but rather the loosening of controls over children's movements. While substance-affected children need structure, this can be provided through adult facilitation and consistency of responses, rather than through the activities themselves (see Figure 6.5).

Children can be afforded feelings of control and belonging through the use of a more relaxed schedule and with greater use of "free choice" activities. This means preparing the environment and allowing children to select the activities they want to be involved in. A single, adult-planned activity might be included for each day, along with the timely meeting of children's physical needs for food, water, sleep, and elimination. Children will gradually develop responsible and appropriate behaviors if they are offered choices and guidelines for wise exercise of those choices.

Defining Program Success

When working with damaged and high-risk populations it is normal to look for indications of success with clients. Intensive involvement with addicted and recovering parents *and* their children is relatively new, and standardized measures of success have yet to be identified. When dealing with human beings, however, looking for predetermined changes may be a mistake. Neither adults nor children change in predictable or uniform ways. One step forward may be followed by two steps backward. An addicted parent needs to learn self-care and nurturance before being able to care effectively for her children. It may be a long time, if ever, before she can actively support all the goals of the child development program.

There are some ways, however, of defining program success that are realistic. Together with case workers or teachers (where applicable), parents can set some goals of their own for the growth of their parental competence. A series of simple, easy-to-complete tasks should accompany each goal. For example, a parent might set a goal of becoming more attentive to her child's needs. To achieve this she would work on tasks such as stopping as many times to listen to her child as possible, when her child calls, "Mommy!" She would also try to plan 15 minutes of uninterrupted time per day with her child. During this time she would not answer the phone or talk to another adult. Both client and professional can feel a sense of accomplishment as these objectives are met.

Tasks for child development should be measured in even smaller increments. Approximations of hoped-for behavior or short-lived periods of change should be accepted as indications of growth. As small movements occur, the child should be rewarded and made aware that adults have noticed his or her efforts.

By recognizing small and gradual changes professionals can be energized to feel that they do make a difference and can handle the disappointments associated with setbacks. At the same time, it must be understood that we can never fully understand, nor can we exactly measure the impact that we have on others. As professionals, we should never underestimate the power of our best efforts.

Figure 6.5

Sample Morning Schedule (regular classroom)	Sample Morning Schedule (classroom that includes substance-affected children)
7:00–9:00 Arrival of children; breakfast; free-choice activities	7:00–9:00 Arrival of children; breakfast; free-choice activities
9:00–9:30 Circle Time	9:00–9:45 Activity Time
9:30–9:45 Story Time	9:45–10:00 Story Time
9:45–10:00 Toileting	10:00–10:15 Toileting
10:00–10:30 Snack Time	10:15–10:35 Snack Time
10:30–11:00 Activity Time	10:35–11:45 Free-choice or outdoor play time
11:00–11:45 Free-choice or outdoor play time	
11:45–12:00 Toileting	11:45–12:00 Toileting
12:00–12:30 Lunch	12:00–12:30 Lunch

Resources

Brickman, N., and L. Taylor (Eds.). *Supporting Young Learners*. Ypsilanti, MI: High/Scope Press, 1991.

Cherry, C., et al. *Nursery School and Day Care Management Guide*, Second Edition. Belmont, CA: David S. Lake Publishers, 1987.

Click, P.M., and D.W. Click. *Administration of Schools for Young Children*, Third Edition. New York: Delmar Publishers, 1990.

Coakley, B., and M. Kopp. *Guide to Establishing and Operating Day Care Centers for Young Children*. Washington, DC: Child Welfare League of America, 1991.

Essa, E.L. *Practical Guide to Solving Preschool Behavior Problems*, Second Edition. New York: Delmar Publishers, 1990.

Essa, E.L., and P.R. Rogers. *Early Childhood Curriculum: From Developmental Model to Application*. New York: Delmar Publishers, Inc, 1992.

Gestwicki, C. *Developmentally Appropriate Practice*. New York: Delmar Publishers, 1995.

Herbert, J.E., M. O'Brien, J. Porterfield and T.R. Risley. *The Infant Center: A Complete Guide to Organizing and Managing Infant Day Care*. Austin, TX: PRO-ED, Inc., 1977.

Hildebrand, V. *Management of Child Development Centers*. Second Edition. Indianapolis, IN: Macmillan Publishing Company, Inc., 1990.

Kostelnick, M.J., et al. *Guiding Children's Social Development: Classroom Practices*. Second Edition. New York: Delmar Publishers, 1993.

Program Implementation Profile: Administration Manual. Ypsilanti, MI: High/Scope Press, 1989.

Schweenhart, L.J. *A School Administrators Guide to Early Childhood Education Programs*. Ypsilanti, MI: High/Scope Press, 1988.

Sciarra, D.J., and A.G. Dorsey. *Developing and Administering a Child Day Care Center*. Third Edition. Albany, NY: Delmar Publishers, Inc., 1995.

Watkins, K.P., and L. Durant. *The Complete Book of Forms for Managing the Early Childhood Program*. West Nyack, NY: Center for Applied Research in Education/Simon and Schuster, 1990.

Watkins, K.P., and L. Durant. *The Complete Early Childhood Behavior Management Guide*. West Nyack, NY: Center for Applied Research in Education/Simon and Schuster, 1992.

Watkins, K.P., and L. Durant. *The Preschool Director's Staff Development Handbook*. West Nyack, NY: Center for Applied Research in Education/Simon and Schuster, 1987.

CHAPTER SEVEN

Activities for Parent Education and Child Development

There is an increasing need for programs that serve young children to also assist the family unit. Young parents lack much-needed support systems, and can become confused by the dearth of information available on child rearing. Parents do need help from professionals, but not always the traditional kind. The most effective specialists do not push their expertise on families. Instead, they help parents to recognize their own strengths and to build on them. Contact with people in the helping professions should make mothers and fathers feel *more* competent, not less so.

Some schools see the classroom as an environment completely separate from the home. It is a place devoted to academics, where the teacher is in charge. Early childhood and intervention programs have taken an approach to their work with families that is different from that found in many other educational settings. In these places, it is understood that the child is innately intertwined with his or her parents. Caregivers and teachers recognize that without parental understanding and support of the program, the benefits to the child will be limited. Furthermore, if the child's home circumstances are unsafe, unhealthy, or otherwise detrimental, he or she may not be able to make full use of the schooling. Therefore, professionals work to help parents understand the rationale behind the program, while helping to meet the family's basic needs.

A program that works with many types of families, including those affected by substance abuse, attempts to support the development of parents and children. Staff members recognize that children are with them for only a short period. Mothers, fathers, and grandparents are the primary caretakers now and into the future. Through their contact with programs, families should be stronger.

In this chapter we provide a series of 30 sample activities for use in programs serving young children and their parents. They are divided into three types: activities for parent support or education; activities to facilitate child development; and those for the parent-child dyad. Readers should note that the activities are not aimed specifically at families affected by substance abuse. Instead they were selected because they address the development of many different families. The outcomes include making participants feel good about themselves, facilitating language skills, and developing family identity. These are goals that should exist for all parents and children.

"We Are a Family"

TYPE OF ACTIVITY: Parent Education

GOAL OF ACTIVITY: To help parents develop awareness of the many things they have in common with other family members, including their children

NUMBER OF PARTICIPANTS: 10–12 parents

MATERIALS NEEDED: Newsprint, magic markers, masking tape

PROCEDURES TO BE FOLLOWED:　Each parent will take a sheet of newsprint and tape it to the wall. Using a magic marker each writes his or her family name on the top of the sheet, that is, "Smith Family." Underneath, the names of family members are listed with space left in between each name. The facilitator then goes around the circle of parents, asking each to select a family member and describe what he or she has in common with that person. If the parent has difficulty thinking of similarities, other group members can assist. Commonalties should be listed on the newsprint next to that person's name. The focus should be on shared positive traits and strengths.

FOLLOW-UP NOTES: Suggest that each parent take the newsprint sheet home to share with family members.

© 1996 by The Center for Applied Research in Education

"My Family Portrait"

TYPE OF ACTIVITY: Parent Education

GOAL OF ACTIVITY: To provide an opportunity for parents to use art materials to express feelings about family, and to provide an outlet for creative expression

NUMBER OF PARTICIPANTS: 10–15 parents

MATERIALS NEEDED: Oaktag or other heavy art paper, old magazines, scissors, glue, magic markers, old photographs of family members, collected collage materials

PROCEDURES TO BE FOLLOWED: Provide tables and chairs where parents can work. The facilitator will introduce the activity by stressing the uniqueness of each family. Then ask the parents to use the materials provided to create their own family portraits. Suggest portraying each member in ways and settings that are special to that person.

FOLLOW-UP NOTES: Using construction paper, frame the family portraits for display at home.

"I Like You, Because . . ."

TYPE OF ACTIVITY: Parent Education

GOAL OF ACTIVITY: To build parental self-esteem through peer feedback

NUMBER OF PARTICIPANTS: 10–15 parents

MATERIALS NEEDED: Newsprint, magic markers, masking tape

PROCEDURES TO BE FOLLOWED: Have parents sit in a circle. Each hangs a sheet of newsprint on the wall and writes his or her name at the top. Going around the circle, the facilitator asks the parents to take turns naming a positive trait of another group member. For example: "I like Joan, because she is always kind to me." Each comment is listed on that person's sheet of newsprint.

FOLLOW-UP NOTES: Ask parents to do this activity at home with their children, and to display the sheets where children can see them.

© 1996 by The Center for Applied Research in Education

JOAN
1. I like Joan because she is always kind to me.
2. I like Joan because she listens to me.
3. I like Joan because she makes me feel important.
4. I like Joan because she is open + caring.
5. I like Joan because she has a sense of humor.
6. I like Joan because she is smart.

"Parents' Beauty Makeover Day"

TYPE OF ACTIVITY: Parent Education

GOAL OF ACTIVITY: To raise parental self-esteem and highlight the need for care of the self and occasional pampering

NUMBER OF PARTICIPANTS: Dependent on space and availability of volunteers

MATERIALS NEEDED: Supplies for hair cutting and styling and manicures; table for arranging supplies; mirrors; radio or tape player and tapes; refreshments

PROCEDURES TO BE FOLLOWED: Volunteers for this activity can be sought from local beauty culture schools. Advise parents in advance of this activity, using announcement posters with attached appointment sign-up sheets. Schedule appointments approximately one-half hour apart. Ask parents to arrive with freshly shampooed hair. Have a space or room set up to provide a degree of privacy during hair cutting and manicures. Provide background music and light refreshments. Offer lunch and letters documenting volunteer service to the volunteers.

FOLLOW-UP NOTES: Take instant photographs of parents with new hairstyles and create an "Our Beautiful/Handsome Parents" display.

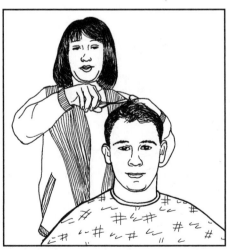

111

"Mock Classroom"

TYPE OF ACTIVITY: Parent Education

GOAL OF ACTIVITY: To help parents develop appreciation of the types of activities that are a part of their children's school day

NUMBER OF PARTICIPANTS: 8–10 parents

MATERIALS NEEDED: Classroom or playroom set up for early childhood education activities, such as block play, sociodramatic play, art activities, and motor skills development

PROCEDURES TO BE FOLLOWED: Have the parents, in small groups, follow a shortened version of their children's daily schedule. Sample activities might include: water play, a music and movement experience, an art activity, and a food preparation experience. As parents are involved in the various activities, the facilitator will briefly explain some of the developmental benefits to the children and answer parents' questions.

FOLLOW-UP NOTES: Have parents put their names on their artwork and take finished projects home to display.

© 1996 by The Center for Applied Research in Education

"To Market, to Market"

TYPE OF ACTIVITY: Parent Education

GOAL OF ACTIVITY: To help parents develop skills for managing children's behavior

NUMBER OF PARTICIPANTS: 10-15 parents

MATERIALS NEEDED: Newsprint, magic markers, masking tape

PROCEDURES TO BE FOLLOWED: The facilitator will hang three sheets of newsprint on the wall and label them as follows: "Problems," "Causes," and "Solutions." Using a trip to the supermarket as an example of an "adult" outing, ask parents to compile a list of the problems encountered when they have to take their children grocery shopping with them. Examples of problems might include: whining, asking for favorite foods, quarreling, or hitting siblings. Discuss the possible causes of problems, such as hunger, fatigue, or boredom. Finally, generate a list of solutions, for example, carrying baggies with favorite snacks or giving the child an illustrated shopping list of his or her own.

FOLLOW-UP NOTES: Ask parents to try some of the solutions on their next market trip and to report back to the group.

"Parents as Storytellers"

TYPE OF ACTIVITY: Parent Education

GOAL OF ACTIVITY: To give parents tools for developing children's emerging literacy

NUMBER OF PARTICIPANTS: 10–15 parents

MATERIALS NEEDED: Golden Books or other inexpensive copies of familiar childhood stories; sheets of flannel in various colors; paper templates depicting story characters and props; magic markers; scissors; glue; ziplock sandwich bags

PROCEDURES TO BE FOLLOWED: The facilitator will read several of the books aloud to the assembled parents. Explain how the flannel board can be used to tell a story without a book. Demonstrate using a completed set of flannel board story pieces. Introduce the parents to the materials for making their own flannel board stories. Ask parents to select their favorite book and to make the pieces needed. Provide ziplock baggies so that parents can take the story pieces home with them.

FOLLOW-UP NOTES: Ask several parents to practice telling their stories to the group, and all parents to try telling their stories to their children.

© 1996 by The Center for Applied Research in Education

"How My Baby Grows"

TYPE OF ACTIVITY: Parent Education

GOAL OF ACTIVITY: To facilitate parents' understanding of child development by charting milestones as they occur in the first five years of life

NUMBER OF PARTICIPANTS: 10–15 parents

MATERIALS NEEDED: Large sheets of drawing paper, magic markers, stapler and staples, old parenting magazines, glue, scissors

PROCEDURES TO BE FOLLOWED: This activity is to be completed over five sessions. The facilitator will explain to parents that they will be making their own child development books. Parents will begin by preparing the books. Six sheets of paper should be put into one pile, folded down the center, then stapled on the fold. Parents can select and write their own titles on the book covers, such as "Mom's Book About Johnny." Each of the right-hand inside pages should then be headed as follows: "When Johnny was a newborn . . . When Johnny was one . . . When Johnny was two . . .," etc. In this and each of the four following sessions the facilitator will discuss the milestones that occur during the years from 1 to 5. At the end of that session, the parents use magazine photos to illustrate the appropriate page and to write down the information learned about the child at that age.

FOLLOW-UP NOTES: Ask parents to share the completed books with spouses or partners and their children.

"The Family That Reads Together"

TYPE OF ACTIVITY: Parent Education

GOAL OF ACTIVITY: To demonstrate for parents the use of the library as a setting for teaching appropriate social-behavioral skills and to stress to parents the importance of modeling reading for their children

NUMBER OF PARTICIPANTS: 10–15 parents

MATERIALS NEEDED: A mock library setting with a book display shelf, books, a reading table and chairs, and a book check-out counter

PROCEDURES TO BE FOLLOWED: The facilitator will suggest to parents that reading to children and regular library trips should begin while the child is a toddler. Discuss the benefits of reading aloud and having children become familiar with the library at an early age. Make a list with parents of the types of behavior appropriate in the library, as well as those that children might actually exhibit. Have parents role play scenarios of child behavior in the library and discuss ways of handling that behavior.

FOLLOW-UP NOTES: Ask parents to take their children on trips to get their library cards and to check out books.

"Coping with Parent-Child Separation Anxiety"

TYPE OF ACTIVITY: Parent Education

GOAL OF ACTIVITY: To help parents cope with the problems that arise for both them and their children as a result of separations

NUMBER OF PARTICIPANTS: 10–15 parents

MATERIALS NEEDED: Newsprint, magic markers, masking tape

PROCEDURES TO BE FOLLOWED: The facilitator will hang four sheets of newsprint on the wall and label these as follows: "When I am away from my child I . . ." "When I leave my child he/she . . ." "I would feel better about leaving my child if..." and "I can help my child cope with separation by . . ." Begin by discussing with parents what their fears are about separations from their children (child may get hurt, parent may miss important milestones in development, child may become too attached to the other caretaker). Ask parents to describe their children's reactions to separations (refusing to eat, screaming, tantrums, withdrawal, indifference). Solicit opinions about what things would make separations easier for both them and for their children (reassurance from caregiver, chances to check on the child's well-being, information updates on the child's day, letting child bring a favorite toy or lovey from home, one-to-one attention for the child from the caregiver). Emphasize the normalcy of separation anxiety for both parent and child.

FOLLOW-UP NOTES: Ask parents to try techniques for easing separation anxiety and to report back to the group.

"Everybody's Birthday"

TYPE OF ACTIVITY: Child Development

GOAL OF ACTIVITY: To help children develop self-worth, and to develop a sense of belonging among group members

NUMBER OF PARTICIPANTS: Entire class or group of children—suitable for children from 2 to 8 years

MATERIALS NEEDED: Microwaveable cupcakes (enough for all children and adults present), birthday candles/hats/napkins/plates/cups, juice or milk, age-appropriate wrapped party favors, Polaroid camera and film

PROCEDURES TO BE FOLLOWED: The facilitator should announce to the children the day before that tomorrow will be "Everybody's Birthday." At midmorning on the party day, the children will assist in mixing the microwave cupcake batter and spooning it into the baking tray. After the facilitator bakes the cupcakes and they cool, the children will ice them. Before party time, the adult will put a birthday candle into each cupcake. At lunch time, the children help to set the table with the birthday tableware, hats, and utensils. After eating lunch each of the children receives a birthday cupcake and all sing "Happy Birthday to Us." After candles are blown out, the children open their party favors, and each has a birthday photograph taken.

FOLLOW-UP NOTES: Make an "Everybody's Birthday" poster or bulletin board using the children's photographs and other shots from the party. After ample display send the photos home to the parents.

"Feelings Wall"

TYPE OF ACTIVITY: Child Development

GOAL OF ACTIVITY: To promote children's positive expression of feelings and emotions

NUMBER OF PARTICIPANTS: Entire class or group of children—suitable for children from 5 to 8 years

MATERIALS NEEDED: Large, long sheets of brown or white wrapping paper, various art materials (paint and brushes, markers, crayons, pencils, fingerpaint)

PROCEDURES TO BE FOLLOWED: The facilitator will tape large sheets of wrapping paper together to form a large writing/drawing surface, then tape these to the wall at the children's eye level. Ideally, the surface should be 6 to 8 feet long and 3 feet high. Explain to the children that any time they have special feelings (joy, anger, love, sadness), they can use the "Feelings Wall" and the art materials to express them in words or pictures. The adult can demonstrate by being the first to write on the wall.

FOLLOW-UP NOTES: Take a trip to the library with the children to find and check out books on feelings.

"Monster Mash"

TYPE OF ACTIVITY: Child Development

GOAL OF ACTIVITY: To reduce children's stress and promote fine motor skills

NUMBER OF PARTICIPANTS: Entire class broken into groups of four to six children each—suitable for children from 2 to 8 years

MATERIALS NEEDED: Boxes of cornstarch, small pitchers of warm water, mixing bowls and spoons (one for each group), green food coloring, shallow trays or cookie sheets (one for every two children), smocks

PROCEDURES TO BE FOLLOWED: Have children wash hands, then gather them around the tables. The facilitator will explain that the children will be making some "Monster Mash, " and it will be fun to play in. Cover the children's clothing with smocks and roll up their sleeves. Have each group open a box of cornstarch, pour it into a mixing bowl, and slowly add warm water until a rubbery-feeling substance results. Adults will know that the mixture is ready when it leaves a clean spot when scraped from the sides of the bowl with the fingers. It will also seem powdery when squeezed, then return to liquid as it drips from the fingers. Add several drops of green food coloring to the prepared mixture. If too wet, add more cornstarch. If the mixture seems to get dry, add a bit more water. Put the "Monster Mash" on trays, and have the children put their hands in.

FOLLOW-UP NOTES: Send the recipe home with the children for parents to try.

© 1996 by The Center for Applied Research in Education

"Crinkled Paper Balls"

TYPE OF ACTIVITY: Child Development

GOAL OF ACTIVITY: To provide stress reduction and opportunities for motor skills development

NUMBER OF PARTICIPANTS: Entire class or group of children—suitable for children from 2 to 8 years

MATERIALS NEEDED: Newspaper, masking tape, magic markers

PROCEDURES TO BE FOLLOWED: Gather the children together at tables. Explain that they will be making their own balls for play inside and outdoors. Have the children crinkle sheets or strips of newspaper into tight ball shapes. Then they will cover the balls with strips of masking tape that they or the adults have torn from the roll. When the balls are completely covered the facilitator can organize and get the children involved in games—catch, keep away, relay races. Balls are safe for the classroom or playground.

FOLLOW-UP NOTES: Have the children decorate individual balls with nontoxic, waterproof markers.

"Bath Time"

TYPE OF ACTIVITY: Child Development

GOAL OF ACTIVITY: To promote cleanliness and self-care skills among children

NUMBER OF PARTICIPANTS: Small groups of four to six children—suitable for children from 2 to 8 years

MATERIALS NEEDED: Small tubs or basins; rubber baby dolls preferably with rooted, washable hair; travel sizes of soap/baby shampoo/powder; washcloths and hand towels (one per child)

PROCEDURES TO BE FOLLOWED: Have the children cover their clothing and tell them that the doll babies need to be bathed. Remind children both before and after that only adults bathe real babies. Fill the basins to the one-half point with warm water and have the children undress the dolls. Explain that the dolls should be washed with the washcloth and soap. Point out that arms, legs, trunk, and face should be cleaned. Have the children shampoo the dolls' hair, rinse, dry, and powder the babies before redressing them.

FOLLOW-UP NOTES: Have a Follow-Up discussion about washing our own bodies and hair.

© 1996 by The Center for Applied Research in Education

"Our Book of Friends"

TYPE OF ACTIVITY: Child Development

GOAL OF ACTIVITY: To promote caring and friendship among the children, while promoting self-recognition and awareness of others

NUMBER OF PARTICIPANTS: One adult to one child or a small group of four to six children—suitable for children from 12 months to 8 years

MATERIALS NEEDED: Collection of children's photographs from various class activities, photograph album (4" x 5" format)

PROCEDURES TO BE FOLLOWED: The facilitator will prepare the book in advance by placing the accumulated photographs in the album. Then the photos should be labeled with captions and/or the children's names. The completed book can be titled (e.g., "Our Friends") and placed on the library shelf. It can be introduced to the children one by one or in small groups. The adult will ask the children questions about the photos, such as, "Who is in this picture? What are they doing?"

FOLLOW-UP NOTES: Make additional books of children's photographs related to specific activities. Sample books include: "We Go to the Fire Station" and "We Make Peanutbutter."

"Our Story"

TYPE OF ACTIVITY: Child Development

GOAL OF ACTIVITY: To develop children's expressive language skills and cognitive abilities (recall and classifying)

NUMBER OF PARTICIPANTS: Entire class or group of children—suitable for children from 2 to 8 years

MATERIALS NEEDED: Newsprint, magic markers, masking tape, photographs of children (optional)

PROCEDURES TO BE FOLLOWED: On the day after a field trip or special event, the facilitator will gather the children together in a circle. Remind the children about the trip, and ask them to tell their version of it. The adult will not expect the children to remember events in order, as this is not a skill of children in the early childhood period. As children describe the event, the adult will use newsprint to record exactly what each child says about it. For example: Patty said, "We rode on the school bus." Print the children's remarks neatly using both upper- and lower-case letters. Read the completed story aloud to the children, pointing to each child's statement as it is read.

FOLLOW-UP NOTES: Illustrate the story with pictures taken on the trip, and post it for parents and visitors to read.

"We Make Dessert"

TYPE OF ACTIVITY: Child Development

GOAL OF ACTIVITY: To promote children's roles as family and school group members, and to facilitate the growth of social skills of sharing and cooperation

NUMBER OF PARTICIPANTS: Small groups of four to six children—suitable for children from 3 to 8 years

MATERIALS NEEDED: Boxes of instant pudding (any flavor), milk, mixing bowl and spoon, measuring cup, six-ounce paper cups, aluminum foil, rubber bands, lunch-size paper bags, smocks

PROCEDURES TO BE FOLLOWED: Have children wash hands and don smocks. The facilitator will explain that they will be making dessert for their families. Have children combine pudding and milk, stirring until ready. Children will spoon pudding into paper cups up to the midpoint, cover with foil and circle with a rubber band. Children will put enough pudding cups into lunch bags to serve one to each person in their families. Adult will label the bags with the children's names and refrigerate until the end of the day.

FOLLOW-UP NOTES: Substitute a quick bread mix for the pudding to make another take-home dessert.

"Happy Mother's/Father's Day"

TYPE OF ACTIVITY Child Development

GOAL OF ACTIVITY: To help children prepare a gift to show appreciation for a parent, and to raise children's self-esteem

NUMBER OF PARTICIPANTS: Small group of four to six children—suitable for children from 3 to 8 years

MATERIALS NEEDED: Smocks, flat of small flowering plants, potting soil, individual planters, popsicle sticks, spoons, watering can, ribbon

PROCEDURES TO BE FOLLOWED: Have children wash hands, don smocks, and gather around a table. Explain to them that they will be potting plants for Mother's or Father's Day. Show children how to select and remove a plant from the flat. Using spoons, have children put a small amount of potting soil into their planters. Then the children should set their plants into the planters and cover the roots with soil. Children's names should be put on popsicle sticks, and the sticks inserted into the soil of the planters. Children will place their plants in a sunny location and water them. To assure that each child has a growing plant, put some plants aside.

FOLLOW-UP NOTES: Before presenting plants to parents, have children circle the planter with a ribbon.

© 1996 by The Center for Applied Research in Education

"Our Classroom Rules"

TYPE OF ACTIVITY: Child Development

GOAL OF ACTIVITY: To promote the development of age-appropriate social skills and classroom behaviors

NUMBER OF PARTICIPANTS: Entire class or group of children—suitable for children from 2 to 8 years

MATERIALS NEEDED: A poster-size, illustrated chart of classroom rules

PROCEDURES TO BE FOLLOWED: The facilitator will prepare the rules chart ahead of time, keeping the following principles in mind: Rules should be stated in the positive. They should be age-appropriate. Rules should number no more than five. Both upper- and lower-case letters should be used. Rules should be illustrated with carefully selected pictures. Rules should be prominently displayed at the children's eye level. When introducing the rules to the children, the adult should gather them in a circle near the chart. Review each rule, focusing on the pictures as a way for children to recall what the rule says. Rules should be regularly reviewed.

SAMPLE RULES

- We hug and pat friends gently.
- We share with friends.
- We wait for our turn.
- We put toys away after play.
- If someone hurts us, we tell a grownup.

FOLLOW-UP NOTES: Have the children develop rules for specific areas of the classroom, such as "Block Corner Rules" or "Our Library Rules." Illustrate and post these in the appropriate areas.

"Green Eggs and Ham"

TYPE OF ACTIVITY: Parent and Child Experience

GOAL OF ACTIVITY: To promote children's language development, and to help parents recognize food preparation activities as positive social and learning experiences

NUMBER OF PARTICIPANTS: Four parents and their children—suitable for children from 3 to 8 years

MATERIALS NEEDED: Ham slices, eggs, skillet, no-stick cooking spray, green food coloring, spatula, whisk, mixing bowl and spoon, plates, eating utensils, smocks, and copy of Dr. Seuss's *Green Eggs and Ham*

PROCEDURES TO BE FOLLOWED: The facilitator will read the book *Green Eggs and Ham* to the assembled parents and children. Then all wash hands and don smocks to protect clothing. Facilitator asks children if they know what green eggs and ham taste like and if they would like to try them. Parents and children crack eggs and put them into a bowl, where they whip the eggs and add several drops of green food coloring. Each parent and child will take a turn frying the ham slice and scrambling the eggs in the skillet. Adults should emphasize that only adults use the electric skillet.

FOLLOW-UP NOTES: After preparing the food, parents and children will sit down together to share their meal. Milk, fruit, and toast can be added to the menu.

© 1996 by The Center for Applied Research in Education

"Learning About Playground Safety"

TYPE OF ACTIVITY: Parent and Child Experience

GOAL OF ACTIVITY: To assist parents in the development of skills to protect child health and safety and to help children understand the importance of outdoor safety

NUMBER OF PARTICIPANTS: Five parents and their children—suitable for children from 2 to 8 years

MATERIALS NEEDED: First-aid kit, drinking water and cups, healthy snacks, tissues, tags with children's names/addresses/telephone numbers

PROCEDURES TO BE FOLLOWED: The facilitator will gather parents together first for a brief discussion of playground safety issues. Generate a list of potential safety problems (falls from swings or sliding board, broken glass, etc.), as well as items that should be taken on the trip (first-aid kit, drinking water, tissues, etc.). Have parents suggest ways to keep children safe. Discuss the playground rules with the children. Then put on name tags and walk to the playground.

SAMPLE RULES

- Hold an adult's hand on the way to the playground.
- Only one child on the slide at a time.
- Walk far away from swings when other children are on them
- Stay inside of the playground fence.

FOLLOW-UP NOTES: Meet with parents the following day to evaluate the safety of the trip. Discuss ways to make the next trip safer for the children.

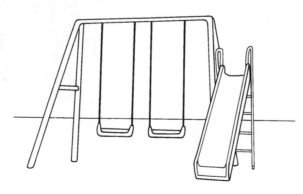

129

"Me and My Shadow"

TYPE OF ACTIVITY: Parent and Child Experience

GOAL OF ACTIVITY: To provide opportunities for the growth of parent and child self-esteem and to offer a project for parent and child to complete together

NUMBER OF PARTICIPANTS: Four parents and their children—suitable for children from 3 to 8 years

MATERIALS NEEDED: A large roll of brown wrapping paper, magic markers, crayons, scissors, glue, yarn in various colors, pieces of scrap material, masking tape

PROCEDURES TO BE FOLLOWED: The facilitator will explain to the assembled parents and children that they will be making self-portraits. Each parent and child team will receive two pieces of brown paper, approximately six feet long by three feet wide. Each parent will ask his/her child to lie on the paper, and the adult will trace around the child's body. The child will also trace around the parent, using the second piece of paper. Using the yarn for hair and material for clothing, the parent-child teams will complete their portraits by drawing in features.

FOLLOW-UP NOTES: The parent and child portraits will be hung in the classroom or hallway side by side, labeled with their names, for example, "Rachel and Mom."

"We Paint with Pudding"

TYPE OF ACTIVITY: Parent and Child Experience

GOAL OF ACTIVITY: To provide parents and children together with an opportunity for creative expression and relaxation

NUMBER OF PARTICIPANTS: Five parents and their children—suitable for children from 1 to 8 years

MATERIALS NEEDED: Instant vanilla-flavored pudding, milk, mixing bowl and spoon, food coloring (various colors), paper cups, plastic teaspoons, butcher or finger paint paper

PROCEDURES TO BE FOLLOWED: The facilitator will explain to parents and children that they will be using pudding to finger paint. Together they will mix the instant pudding and put small amounts into paper cups. Different colors will be added to the cups to make a variety of shades of pudding paint. Then each participant will spoon some pudding onto the finger paint paper, and use his or her finger to make designs and pictures. Children and adults can taste as they paint.

FOLLOW-UP NOTES: Display the finished paintings prominently, along with the artists' names.

"Our Holiday Celebration"

TYPE OF ACTIVITY: Parent and Child Experience

GOAL OF ACTIVITY: To support families in the celebration of the holiday season, while developing a sense of community and belonging among everyone in the program

NUMBER OF PARTICIPANTS: All interested parents and children in the program—suitable for all age groups

MATERIALS NEEDED: An Advent wreath, a Menorah, a kinara; age-appropriate children's books about Christmas, Hanukkah, and Kwanza; foods to accompany each celebration

PROCEDURES TO BE FOLLOWED: This activity occurs as a series of events over three days. Parents should be asked to be involved ahead of time and to contribute food. The facilitator will explain to the parents that through this type of celebration everyone's holiday can be acknowledged, and children can develop an appreciation for the religion and culture of others. This will be accomplished through the lighting of ceremonial candles, something that the celebrations have in common. Prepare the children by telling them that there will be three days of winter holiday celebrations. On day one, light the candles on the Advent wreath, read a Christmas story, and share cocoa and cookies. On day two, light the candles on the Menorah, read a Hanukkah story, and share latkes and grape juice. On day three, light the candles on the kinara, read a Kwanza story, and share fresh fruits and vegetables.

FOLLOW-UP NOTES: Take photographs of the celebrations and make a display for children, parents, and visitors to see.

"Story Hour"

TYPE OF ACTIVITY: Parent and Child Experience

GOAL OF ACTIVITY: To help parents develop skills for reading aloud to their children, and to promote children's language development

NUMBER OF PARTICIPANTS: Five parents and their children—suitable for children from birth to age 8

MATERIALS NEEDED: A selection of age-appropriate children's books, comfortable chairs or floor cushions

PROCEDURES TO BE FOLLOWED: The facilitator will introduce the activity by reading one book to the assembled group. He or she will model read-aloud skills, such as holding the book so listeners can see the pictures, using facial and verbal expression, and asking and answering questions. Then parents will be invited to take turns reading other books to the group.

FOLLOW-UP NOTES: Ask parents to read aloud to their children at home and report back to the parents' group on their success.

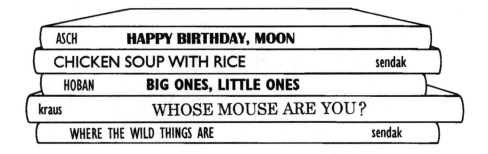

"My Chores Chart"

TYPE OF ACTIVITY: Parent and Child Experience

GOAL OF ACTIVITY: To help parents develop a mechanism for reinforcing rules and children's responsibilities as family members

NUMBER OF PARTICIPANTS: Five parents and their children—suitable for children from 4 to 8 years

MATERIALS NEEDED: Poster board (five sheets), rulers, magic markers, old magazines, scissors, glue, colorful stickers

PROCEDURES TO BE FOLLOWED: The facilitator explains to the parents and children that the group will begin with a discussion of things that family members do to help one another. For example, mothers often cook meals and do laundry for the rest of the family. Ask parents what jobs they want their children to do at home. Sample chores for young children might include: cleaning up toys, setting the table, or feeding pets. Working together, parents and children will make "Chores Charts." They will list the jobs that parents want children to complete on a daily or weekly basis. Pictures will be cut from magazines to illustrate each chore. Families will receive stickers to use to indicate that a child has completed a job.

FOLLOW-UP NOTES: Ask parents to display the completed charts at home, and to report back on the success associated with using them.

"Fun Dough Bakery"

TYPE OF ACTIVITY: Parent and Child Experience

GOAL OF ACTIVITY: To develop parent and child cooperation and sharing, and to reduce stress

NUMBER OF PARTICIPANTS: Five parents and their children—suitable for children from 2 to 8 years

MATERIALS NEEDED: Six cups flour, two cups salt, two cups water, one cup vegetable oil, mixing bowl and spoon, rolling pin, cookie cutters, plastic knives/forks/spoons, empty margarine containers with lids

PROCEDURES TO BE FOLLOWED: The facilitator will introduce the fun dough experience by having an illustrated recipe written on newsprint. Parents and children will add ingredients and mix together. Flour and salt should be combined first. Then oil and water should be added gradually. The mixture must then be kneaded until smooth. If it is too greasy or wet, add a small amount of additional flour. Distribute cookie cutters, rolling pins, and utensils to press dough into interesting shapes.

FOLLOW-UP NOTES: Follow with sociodramatic play using a table as a counter, a toy cash register, and baggies and paper bags in order to have a bakery. Send dough home in margarine containers for continuing parent-child play.

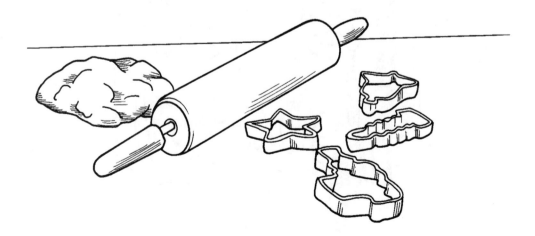

"Puppet Show"

TYPE OF ACTIVITY: Parent and Child Experience

GOAL OF ACTIVITY: To facilitate self-expression and expressive language skills in both parents and children

NUMBER OF PARTICIPANTS: Five parents and their children—suitable for children from 3 to 8 years

MATERIALS NEEDED: Old socks, mittens, paper sandwich bags, scissors, yarn, glue, magic markers, buttons, felt scraps

PROCEDURES TO BE FOLLOWED: The facilitator will introduce the idea of a parent-and-child puppet show. Each parent-and-child team will select a favorite story, song, or nursery rhyme, and make several characters to go along with it. The facilitator will drape a table with an old sheet to use as a puppet theater. Each parent and child will entertain others in the group using their puppets.

FOLLOW-UP NOTES: Have parents and children sit in a circle and sing favorite songs using their puppets.

"Letters to Home"

TYPE OF ACTIVITY: Parent and Child Experience

GOAL OF ACTIVITY: To promote self-expression, language development, and family literacy skills

NUMBER OF PARTICIPANTS: Five parents and their children—suitable for children from 2 to 8 years

MATERIALS NEEDED: Old greeting cards, drawing paper, scissors, glue, magic markers, crayons, pencils, envelopes, and postage stamps

PROCEDURES TO BE FOLLOWED: The facilitator will explain that parents and children will be making cards to send to one another. Pair off each adult with another parent's child so that the contents of the cards will be a surprise. Demonstrate how to fold drawing paper twice and decorate with greeting card pictures to make original cards. Each adult will write a message to his or her child, and a message from the child being helped, being sure to use the child's own words. Adults will address their own and the children's cards, and show children where to place the stamps.

FOLLOW-UP NOTES: Take a walk to the mail box or post office to mail the cards.

Resources

FOR PARENT EDUCATION

Barnes, R., and R. Barnes. *We Need to Talk*. Dallas, TX: Word Publishing, 1994.

Bennett, S., and R. Bennett. *Table Talk*. Holbrook, MA: Bob Adams, Inc., 1994.

Brazelton, T.B. *Infants and Mothers: Differences in Development*. New York: A Delta Book, 1969.

Brazelton, T.B. *The Earliest Relationship*. Reading, MA: Addison-Wesley, 1993.

Brazelton, T.B. *Toddlers and Parents: A Declaration of Independence*. New York: Delacorte Press, 1974.

Brazelton, T.B. *To Listen to a Child*. Reading, MA: Addison-Wesley, 1993.

Brazelton, T.B. *Touchpoints*. Reading, MA: Addison-Wesley, 1994.

Clark, J.I. *Self-esteem: A Family Affair*. San Francisco: Harper San Francisco, 1978.

Cooper, G.C. *Guide to Teaching Early Childhood Development: A Comprehensive Curriculum*. Washington, DC: Child Welfare League of America, 1975.

Cooper, G.C. *Parenting Curriculum*. Washington, DC: Child Welfare League of America, 1973.

D'Augelli, J.F., and J.M. Weiner. *Communication and Parenting, Leader Guide*. University Park, PA: Penn State University, 1976.

Dinkmeyer, D., and G.D. McKay. *The Parent's Handbook: Systematic Training for Effective Parenting*. Circle Pines, MN: American Guidance Service, 1989.

Faber, A., and E. Mazlish. *How to Talk So Kids Will Listen and Listen So Kids Will Talk*. New York: Avon Books, 1980.

Faber, A., and E. Mazlish. *Liberated Parents, Liberated Children*. New York: Grosset and Dunlap Publishers, 1974.

Galinsky, E. *The Six Stages of Parenting*. Reading, MA: Addison-Wesley, 1987.

Galvin, K.M., and B.J. Brommel. *Family Communication*. Glenview, IL: Scott, Foresman and Company, 1990.

Gordon, T. *Parent Effectiveness Training*. New York: New American Library, 1975.

Myers, G.E., and M.T. Myers. *The Dynamics of Human Communication*. New York: McGraw-Hill Book Company, 1992.

Siegler, A.L. *What Should I Tell The Kids?* New York: Plume Books, 1993.

Watkins, K.P. *Teaching Healthy Parent-Child Communication: "Are You Listening to Me?"* Philadelphia, PA: Temple University, Center for Social Policy and Community Development, 1994.

For Child Development

Bos, C.S., S. Vaughn, and L.M. Levine. *2 to 6: Instructional Activities for Children at Risk*. Allen, TX: DLM Teaching Resources, 19.

Croft, D.S. *An Activities Handbook for Teachers of Young Children*. Fifth Edition. Boston: Houghton Mifflin, 1990.

Dodge, D.T., and L.J. Colker. *Creative Curriculum for Early Childhood*. Third Edition. Washington, DC: Teaching Strategies, 1992.

Hamilton, D.S., and B.M. Flemming. *Resources for Creative Teaching in Early Childhood Education*, Second Edition. New York: Harcourt Brace Jovanovich, 1990.

Herr, J.A., and Y.R. Libby. *Creative Resources for the Early Childhood Classroom*. Second Edition. Albany, NY: Delmar Publishers, 1995.

Kleinburg, L. (Ed.) *Tell How You Feel: Creating an Awareness of Emotions in a Day Care Setting*. Fairfax,VA: Fairfax County Office for Children in School-age Child Care, October 1988.

Lillie, D.L., and T.M. Sturm. *Carolina Early Learning Activities*. Volumes 1 and 2. New York: Walker and Company, 1987.

Mayersky, M. *Creative Activities for Young Children*. Fifth Edition. Albany, NY: Delmar Publishers, 1995.

Newman, D. *The Early Childhood Teachers Almanac: Activities for Each Month of the Year*. West Nyack, NY: Center for Applied Research in Education/Simon and Schuster, 1984.

Poulsson, E. *Finger Plays for Nursery and Kindergarten*. New York: Dover Publications, Inc., 1971.

Sobut, M.A., and B.N. Bogen. *The Complete Early Childhood Curriculum Resource*. West Nyack, NY: The Center for Applied Research in Education/Simon and Schuster, 1991.

CHAPTER EIGHT

Networking and Advocating with Human Service Delivery Systems

In this volume we have attempted to explore the scope of the substance-abuse problem, its impact on the individual and the family, and some of the strategies for working with parents and children. We have also described some of the possible roles for persons in the human services.

The focus of the final chapter is networking with the systems that serve families in order to advocate for them. Advocacy means speaking out on behalf of, taking the part of others. There may be no other single group of families in the country more in need of this support than those touched by addiction; however, there are problems that stand in the way of that support.

One of the barriers is that those who dedicate themselves to the service of others tend to isolate themselves into singular communities, social workers with social workers, teachers with teachers; they may lack opportunities to interface with colleagues in other professions. They speak their own language, but may be unable to communicate problems and needs to others. They may not be aware of the goals shared with professionals in other fields, persons who could also be strong sources of support.

Many are overwhelmed by a sense of "professional loneliness." Human service jobs are stressful and emotionally tiring. Work frustrations cannot always be shared with family and loved ones, so they may be kept inside. Eventually, many dedicated professionals burn out. Some leave their jobs; some stay on, but may become increasingly isolated from co-workers and clients. The work is no longer the vocation they once felt it to be, but becomes only the generator of a pay check.

Professionals working with substance-affected families are not helped by the pervasive apathy of our society. At times they are faced with overwhelmingly pessimistic input from the media about social problems. Some even get this input from their families. "Why would you want to do *that* kind of work? You know that those people will never appreciate it! And it doesn't pay anything, after all those years you spent in school."

This chapter will look at key aspects of the human service system. We will explore the types of services each provides, possibilities for networking, and roles for professionals. Recognizing avenues for support not only improves services to clients but also helps professionals. In connecting with colleagues and advocating for clients, professionals also advocate for themselves. In this way they find the resources to empower clients to work toward drug-free lives.

The Roles of Advocates

Anyone can advocate for substance-affected families. Having knowledge about and concern for the problem, while speaking out to educate others and effect change is advocacy. Advocates work in substance-abuse treatment, education, health care, social work, and the legal system. They provide services through churches and community groups. They share feelings of compassion and an understanding of the very human conditions influencing families coping with addiction. At the same time, they are honest in their dealings with clients, telling the truth about their perceptions of problems.

Advocates help clients and their families to identify the dilemmas facing them (Figure 8.1). This can be a strenuous undertaking, as clients recovering from addiction may not be able to accept the scope and size of the problems without time and extensive counseling. Many of those affected by substance abuse have few coping skills or outside support systems. When assisting with the problem-solving process only a small series of steps can be planned and taken at one time. Relapse and the accompanying feelings of disappointment, a sense of failure and diminished self-esteem, are often part of the client's gradual recovery.

Many recovering clients have had few success experiences. One reason for this is a lack of self-discipline and skills for organizing and moving toward goals. Addicts also have very low self-esteem. Advocates are often involved in promoting skills development and helping clients learn to handle both successes and setbacks.

Much of what this chapter deals with concerns interface with the many systems that provide programs for substance abusers and their families. Advocates must be instrumental in identifying sources of information and agencies that will meet client needs. Most addicted persons have a broad range of problems, including housing, health, and legal problems. These same difficulties also affect their children and partners. Involvement with the family court, foster care and special education programs is not uncommon.

Advocates also act as resources about addictions for colleagues and others in the community. This is accomplished by membership in professional organizations and community groups, as well as by conference and meeting attendance.

Advocacy cannot be static. It requires one to read continually, talk with colleagues, and find ways of learning more. Advances in treatment, research, and program development must be explored as they arise.

Figure 8.1
Roles for Those Advocating for Substance-Affected Families

- Helping clients and their families to identify problems
- Helping clients develop step-by-step strategies for responding to problems
- Helping clients develop skills for effecting change in their lives
- Identifying sources of information and services to assist clients in the change process
- Helping those who offer ancillary services to better understand the substance-abuse problem
- Speaking out in behalf of clients and their needs to other professionals and the community
- Participating in continuing education activities in order to stay abreast of research, treatment, and programming advances

The Education System: Services Provided

School systems across the United States provide a variety of programs, often reflecting the communities they serve. In addition to elementary and secondary school programs, many districts offer both child day care and Head Start, child development programs that can benefit substance-affected children. Child care centers provide extended hours of custodial care for the children of parents who are employed or involved in training programs. Many serve children from birth to age 5. Some child care centers charge fees based on family income. Meals and snacks are often offered as a part of the service, but offerings can vary from one school district to another.

The Head Start program is funded by the federal government through local agencies. Low-income children from 3 to 5 years receive comprehensive services, including education, health, and nutrition services. Screenings for physical and mental health problems are available. In addition there are social service and parent involvement components. Currently, there are no fees for service. In some areas of the country parent-child educators visit families in their homes, and learning center programs are provided for toddlers. While currently operating during traditional school hours, some Head Start centers are in the process of adding extended hours to meet the needs of parents in education and training programs.

In response to increasing demands, many schools also provide before-and-after school programs. This type of child care is offered for children in kindergarten and the primary grades, usually at an elementary school site. Homework assistance, snacks, and recreation are among the activities.

Many school districts have recognized the importance of responding to community needs. Teen parenting and pregnancy prevention, sex education, parenting skills, and drug and alcohol education programs are among those that respond in some ways to the needs of substance-affected families. A few schools even provide special services to homeless children.

In 1975, Public Law 94-142 was passed. This law grants a free and appropriate education to children identified as having special needs. If parents or professionals suspect a disability, developmental delay, or other problem, the local school district or intermediate unit must provide screening to determine if special programming is needed. Goals and a plan to meet them must then be developed. The child's parents have the right to participate in the planning and raise objections if they feel the child's needs are not being properly addressed. Most districts offer a broad range of learning situations for the children served, and counselors, special education teachers, psychologists. and health care providers are among school employees.

Some public school systems also offer free adult education classes. For persons whose educational level is below the eighth grade, adult basic education is provided, while for those seeking to complete their secondary school education, general education development (G.E.D.) classes are available. Classes may also be offered for those needing to develop English speaking and writing skills. These are called English as a Second Language (E.S.L.) programs. Many addicted persons lack basic education skills and school success experiences, and adult education classes can be extremely helpful to them. In addition, they may have the opportunity to demonstrate the importance of schooling to their children.

If the school district has its own teaching (pedagogical) library, it is generally open to the public. Journals in education, school counseling, and aspects of teaching are usually part of the collections, along with books, newspapers, and educational materials.

NETWORKING WITH EDUCATIONAL SYSTEMS

School district programs and services may be listed in local telephone directories. Many offer brochures to publicize special programs. It may be helpful to request a meeting with a knowledgeable representative of the system. In this way one can get an overview of services and find out about policies on community involvement. Many school systems welcome opportunities for joint projects.

Attending public school board meetings, or reading newspaper accounts of meetings can help develop an understanding of curricular issues, funding concerns and program proposals. Most school districts host or participate in conferences in conjunction with professional organizations. In these settings, one can meet and confer with teachers, counselors, and administrators. Ideas and concerns can be shared with those who have similar interests.

Consider networking with colleges and universities that offer teacher and counselor education programs. Both student teachers and practicum students can make significant contributions to addictions treatment programs that offer parent-child services. Students can bring optimism, enthusiasm and fresh ideas to programs where they volunteer.

ROLES FOR EDUCATION PROFESSIONALS

Until recent years there was little involvement by educators in the drug and alcohol problem. There were some substance-abuse education programs in schools, but these were primarily at the secondary school level, beyond the point where children are most reachable. A great many communities simply felt that substance abuse would not touch their children. As the scope of the drug epidemic became apparent, however, things began to change. Attitudes about alcohol abuse were changed somewhat by groups like Mothers Against Drunk Driving (MADD). Schools began to take a more concerted approach to drug and alcohol education, beginning at the elementary school level.

In recent years education professionals have become involved in drug and alcohol treatment. They are now working as parent educators, and developing programs for substance-exposed children. Their knowledge of child development and programming can be invaluable to a team working on client recovery issues.

Education systems are still lagging behind in some areas. Teachers and administrators must take steps to learn more about addiction and the ways that parental substance abuse impacts on a developing child. While teachers at times rightfully feel overburdened, a new understanding of the educator's role must be forged. If the *whole child*, including the child in the family context, is not understood and responded to by the school, education programs cannot hope to be effective. The problems associated with substance abuse are everyday realities for more than a few American school children. They face domestic violence, child abuse, mental health problems, homelessness, and seriously high levels of stress. Teachers and administrators can not afford to be without this information.

Educators cannot deal with the many problems associated with addiction alone. They must begin to utilize the resources available to them in health care, social work, and law enforcement. With this assistance schools may begin to have the most positive of all outcomes—preventing substance abuse before it starts.

Health Care Systems: Services Provided

Americans are fortunate, in that we have a wide array of health services available to us. Unfortunately, those services do not reach all of those who need them. Some people are not aware of health programs in their area, while others live in a part of the country where there are fewer professionals and facilities to meet health care needs.

In addition to hospital-based services and physicians in private practice, many communities provide clinics. Clinics may be specialized (like those that provide prenatal care), or they may provide generalized services. Clinics often serve low-income families either through Medicaid or a health maintenance organization. Many of those affected by drug and alcohol abuse have occasion to use clinics for their health care services.

To get health care to hard-to-reach populations, some services are home-based or mobile. Home visiting nurses, once a staple only in rural areas, are now busy in urban areas as well. The home-bound elderly and the terminally ill are two groups that receive the services of home-visiting health care workers. Some drug treatment programs also provide visits to new mothers and parenting clients. These can be invaluable, in that they offer opportunities for teaching the client skills in a private setting. The nurse can also see what the home environment is like, and provide suggestions for creating a safer, healthier milieu for children.

A newer way of reaching the community with health care services is the mobile unit or health care van. While some of these provide health screening for specific diseases (like breast cancer), others offer well-baby care and immunizations. These services may be funded by hospitals in conjunction with foundation grants.

Programs for mental health and mental retardation are also provided by the health care system. These programs are generally team efforts involving educators and social work staff as well as health care professionals. When the mental health system was deinstitutionalized, it was replaced with an outpatient treatment system. Many people have concerns that these facilities, bound by laws to protect the rights of patients, are unable to be completely effective in helping people with serious mental health disorders. Further complicating the issues, many addicts also suffer from depression and other emotional problems. Few addiction or mental health treatment facilities are equipped to deal with both sets of problems.

Residential hospice programs are another of the services of the health care system. Many of those with AIDS and some with tuberculosis are being treated in these facilities. In addition to providing round-the-clock nursing care for the terminally ill, many offer grief counseling and support for families of the dying.

Health care professionals are among those at the heart of addictions treatment. It is this system that conducts research, monitors and treats health and nutrition problems, and provides medications to alleviate withdrawal symptoms.

NETWORKING WITH HEALTH CARE SYSTEMS

The health care system can seem inaccessible to persons on the outside. Professionals are perceived as being part of a highly specialized society. There are, however, avenues available for accessing health care professionals and services. One of these is through teaching hospitals.

Teaching hospitals have in-house physician, nursing, dental, or technician programs. They are generally also centers for research, and sometimes for public education. Faculty of these health education programs are sometimes eager for involvement with agencies that can give their students opportunities for hands-on experiences and community service.

Even physicians in private practice can be a source of educational materials and information. Many are deluged by patient education literature (books, pamphlets and posters) from pharmaceutical companies. This is particularly true of pediatricians, who may be only too happy to share this wealth with local agencies. Some physicians also volunteer their time to speak to parent groups or to children.

We also recommend seeking, along with health care providers, joint funding for projects from foundations and government sources. Funding sources are increasingly demanding coordination among agencies providing similar services, and are far less likely than in past years to fund more than one project of the same type in any given locale. One drawback to the success of these projects is that many hospitals and university-based medical programs demand as much as a 50-percent rate for administrative overhead in proposal budgets. These are vague, poorly defined fees for use of facilities, energy, and so forth. These costs can interfere with successful funding, and are an issue that must be dealt with in tight economic times.

While medical and health care conferences are not always open to the public, these too are settings for identifying colleagues and for information gathering. Professional journals and newsletters that describe research findings and health care issues are available in most public libraries.

ROLES FOR HEALTH CARE PROFESSIONALS

As the face of health care in the United States gradually changes, professionals who have previously isolated themselves will increasingly be involved with other disciplines. Already some of these changes are underway. Physician education is slowly changing. Bedside manner and appropriate interface with patients' families is being stressed in some training programs.

Health care providers in general can help by promoting understanding of the common goals of those in human services, especially those working with substance-affected families. Recovery from addiction is never merely a matter of drug withdrawal; it also involves therapy to deal with underlying issues, development of interpersonal and educational competencies, and support for parenting skills and family communication.

Health care providers have always been involved to some degree in schools. It was the school nurses who once, almost exclusively, taught personal hygiene classes and responded to the day-to-day ills of students. The need for health care involvement in education is that much greater today, as we must teach children to cope with parental addiction, and to resist peer pressure to use drugs and alcohol or to engage in unprotected sex. These professionals are needed to participate in the development of curricula for child *and* parent education. There are many parents who feel that sex and drug prevention education are strictly the province of the home. Information should be available to help these parents realize that schools must be involved in the process. Health care professionals at all levels must bring their compassion and expertise to schools and community centers, where it can be utilized by colleagues in other disciplines.

Much of the research that identifies the toxic effects of drugs and points the direction for treatment is conducted by health care providers. Insights must be shared with those outside the medical community. Medical conferences might be restructured to draw a broader range of persons from the human services.

Social Service Systems: Services Provided

The social service system is perhaps the most extensive of the many networks that serve substance-affected families. Unlike education and health care systems, it does not have a single primary function. Instead, the social service system addresses a broad range of human needs.

Social workers and their colleagues are intimately involved in drug and alcohol treatment. They serve as individual case workers, admitting clients to programs and taking psychosocial histories. They provide individual counseling to help clients focus on recovery issues. Social workers conduct groups for persons attempting to achieve and maintain sobriety. Some visit the client in his or her home. The roles played by social service staff in addictions treatment are varied and expansive.

In an attempt to describe some of these services, we have divided them into those that assist the family, those focusing on children, and those working with special populations.

Services to Families

Social service delivery may begin literally at the moment that families are formed. Social workers assist new parents while mother and baby are still in the hospital by helping to arrange payment of hospital bills, donation of car seats, formula, infant equipment, and lease of infant monitoring systems. Some parents rely on adoption agencies to help them start or increase their families. Social service workers screen prospective mothers and fathers, and match babies and children to parents.

Families most often receive support from social service systems in times of crisis. Reports of child abuse and neglect are handled by investigating case workers. When children are endangered by their home situations, the system may place them in protective services settings, such as foster care or group homes. Even when children remain with their parents, it is the social service system that monitors the family and supervises family and individual therapy, as well as parenting skills education.

Unfortunately, many families affected by drug and alcohol addiction are also dealing with violence and spousal or child abuse. Shelters for battered women, hotlines, and family counseling are responses made by the social service system.

At times, parents are unable to meet childrearing and household duties due to illness or unexpected employment situations. In these cases, some cities and counties offer homemaker services. A person trained in homemaking and child care temporarily assumes these duties for the absent or ill parent.

Aid to Families with Dependent Children (AFDC) supports parents by providing money to feed, clothe and shelter minor children. Funds may also be provided for transportation and child care if the parent is in a vocational training or education program. While many Americans are concerned that the use of welfare becomes an intergenerational mode of family income, there are countless parents who have used AFDC as a stepping stone to better their lives and those of their children.

Services to Children

In addition to protective services afforded to abused and neglected children, the social services system also responds to the needs of delinquent and runaway children. Those who develop juvenile problems are often placed in group homes or institutions, rather than being imprisoned. These programs provide opportunities for the child to complete his or her schooling, up to the twelfth grade level, offer recreational activities, and mandate counseling.

Child care programs fell under the auspices of the social service system until the emergence of the early childhood education profession in the early 1970s. Today, social workers continue to engage in client recruitment, admissions, and parent involvement, primarily in federally funded programs. The social service staff are often privy to important details of family life, including substance-abuse problems.

Shelters for the homeless are also under the auspices of the social service system. These facilities often do a great deal more than providing bed and board. Some offer education and training programs, child care, and counseling for residents. Referrals to outside services, such as addictions treatment, are available through some shelters.

Services to Special Populations

Programs for persons with disabilities are available through the social service system. Like health care and education professionals, social workers are involved in mental health/mental retardation programs, rehabilitation, and special needs services. They help clients address psychosocial needs and also play roles in some educational activities.

Through this system senior citizens are served with meals-on-wheels, adult day care and recreation programs, and transportation services. Some of the elderly are also drug and alcohol addicted. As a person ages, nutrition and health needs are less apt to be met. Therefore, contacts with social service agencies and staff become even more critical.

Prison societies provide linkage between incarcerated persons and the community. The inmate programs they offer may include religious services, adult education, recreation, and counseling. They also help to keep lines of communication open between prisoners and their families.

NETWORKING WITH SOCIAL SERVICE SYSTEMS

It is a tremendous challenge to develop knowledge of the social service delivery system in a particular community and state. In addition to agencies and programs that are publicly funded, there are private charitable, private profit-making, and church-related agencies. One way of beginning to understand the system is to use a local directory of services. It is important first, to know the kinds of services that are available, and second, to know who offers each type. The next step should be to telephone specific programs in order to identify a contact person and to get a description of what that agency does. A sample telephone interview form has been included in this chapter (see Figure 8.2).

Attendance at subject conferences can be helpful. These are meetings that concern human services providers in many fields. Often there are discussion and brainstorming sessions, where various points of view are illuminated.

When establishing contacts with interesting and potentially helpful colleagues, arrange visits between the two agencies. Ask to tour their facilities, to meet staff, even attend a staff meeting. Even if at the time it does not seem that this contact can be helpful, follow up with a note of thanks and an occasional telephone call.

Figure 8.2
Network Information Form

Interviewer _____

Date _____

Agency name _____

Address _____

Telephone _____   Contact person _____

Client population served _____

Services provided _____

_____

Geographic area served _____

Client eligibility requirements _____

_____

Services provided for children (if different from above) _____

_____

Ages of children served _____

Hours services are available _____

Sources of referrals _____

Can program refer children directly? _____

Contact person for referrals _____

Once client is referred, will agency exchange pertinent information with this

program? _____

Can a representative from this program arrange to visit the agency?

_____

Days/hours convenient for visits _____

Availability of/accessibility to public transportation _____

_____

ROLES FOR SOCIAL SERVICE PROFESSIONALS

Work in the social services often affords the best opportunity to understand the scope of the substance-abuse problem. Social workers come into contact not only with clients but with their families and friends. They recognize that the impacts of addiction are profound. This is not always understood in quite the same way by professionals whose focus is more singular. Social service professionals realize that responding to only part of the addictions problem usually results in recovery failure. This information must be shared with colleagues in education, health care and the legal professions. Clergy and lay church workers also need a better grasp of the magnitude of this problem.

The Legal System: Services Provided

When one thinks of the legal system, the police department, courts and lawyers immediately come to mind. In fact, there are a number of services and providers that come under the jurisdiction of this system. Families affected by addiction come into contact with many of these.

The legal system is not always involved with families because of crimes. Custody battles, separation and divorce, and lawsuits are also the realm of this system. In many cities lawyers have formed agencies specifically to deal with the problems of particular groups. These consortia may be nonprofit providing free services, or request payment on a sliding scale.

Public interest law centers serve the community by helping to develop policy and laws in response to social problems. These legal groups may be mandated to provide public education seminars and conferences on topics of interest. Some publish their own literature on constitutional rights of citizens.

Many people are unaware that in addition to very visible police departments, there are task forces and special investigations units seeking to put a dent in the drug problem. Some of these officers go undercover to ferret out drug dealers, and every year some give their lives in the service of their communities.

As discussed in Chapter Two, there are special programs for juveniles who have been convicted of crimes. Boot camps and group homes are two of these, along with juvenile detention centers. Most of these facilities provide legal counseling, along with other pertinent services. If a child is considered too young to communicate with the court about matters that concern him, an advocate is appointed for him by the judge. This individual conducts his or her own investigation of the matters at hand and speaks before the court in the child's behalf.

For low-income offenders there are legal aid societies and public defenders to assist with defense and bail funds. After serving time in prison, some inmates are released into halfway houses. These are designed to provide a supervised transition from incarceration to life in the community.

While there has been much negative attention focused on the legal profession, there are many concerned and dedicated officers of the court attempting to positively influence this system; some are even involved in substance-abuse treatment.

NETWORKING WITH LEGAL SYSTEMS

The police department is generally another of the very accessible human service agencies. In many cities, officers are appointed as community liaisons. Their focus is listening and responding to public concerns while promoting the good will of the citizenry. Public relations officers will often visit schools and talk with community groups to answer questions and provide information.

The law projects, public interest legal centers, and legal aid groups are eager to provide information. They can be found listed in telephone directories, sometimes with toll-free numbers. Publications are usually available free of charge.

Some law firms have begun to encourage public service activities. Going beyond the occasional pro bono case, these firms promote volunteerism and mentoring, and make sizable donations to nonprofit agencies. Some have "adopted" schools and student groups. Involvements of this type need to be carefully discussed and planned, but are well worth investigating.

Those seeking to build networks in the legal profession should also make contact with local law schools. Public service projects are not uncommon among law students. Many are altruistic and eager for experiences that can help them build understanding of social problems.

ROLES FOR LEGAL SERVICE PROFESSIONALS

Traditionally, the legal profession has been involved primarily in drug law enforcement. Police officers arrest users, dealers, and traffickers; the courts prosecute them; and the prisons incarcerate them. There should, however, be more roles for legal professionals interested in addictions prevention, treatment, and recovery issues.

For example, it is almost impossible for those in the human services to keep up to date with changes in laws and regulations pertaining to drug enforcement and treatment. This is an area where assistance of those in the legal profession can be invaluable. Lawyers can publish updates aimed at lay persons, and can serve on agency boards of directors, thereby providing insights on issues with which others may lack familiarity.

Some lawyers and police officers have volunteered as tutors and mentors in schools and youth agencies. This is of value because many children who develop substance-abuse problems lack supportive role models or outlets for overwhelming personal and family problems. In the future, a focus on roles in addictions prevention may offer more solutions than extra police officers and additional prisons.

Figure 8.3
Services Provided by Human Service Systems

Education Systems

- elementary and secondary schools
- child day care programs
- Head Start programs
- before/after school programs
- sex education programs
- drug and alcohol education
- teen parenting programs
- screening for exceptionality
- programs for exceptional children
- adult education classes
- educational libraries
- teacher colleges

Social Service Systems

- support for parents of newborns
- adoption services
- child protective services
- parenting education classes
- family therapy
- services to families in their homes
- shelters for battered women
- homemaker services
- Aid to Families with Dependent Children
- delinquent /runaway programs
- child care recruitment/admissions
- senior services
- homeless shelters
- mental health/mental retardation services
- drug/alcohol counseling
- services to inmates
- social work education colleges

Health Care Systems

- hospitals
- community-based clinics
- home visiting
- mobile health care units
- hospice programs
- mental health/mental retardation services
- drug/alcohol treatment
- teaching hospitals
- hospice programs

Legal Service Systems

- courts
- police departments
- law projects
- public interest law centers
- legal aid societies
- group homes/boot camps for juveniles
- public defenders
- halfway houses
- court-appointed advocates
- private law firms
- law schools

Churches and Community Agencies

With the exception of court activities and police work, churches and community-based organizations have been involved in every aspect of human services. They run hospitals, drug treatment programs, recovery support groups, homeless shelters, and foster care agencies. Every problem faced by the substance-affected family is being addressed in some fashion by these groups.

These, too, need to be considered as sources of information and networking. Churches and religious groups bring unique insights to the sometimes neglected spiritual aspects of recovery. Community-based agencies often have an excellent grasp of the effects of drug problems on a particular neighborhood. They know the people using drugs, the dealers, and where drugs are sold. They may be able to organize citizen antidrug groups and aid police in targeting drug dealers. Both churches and community agencies can be invaluable resources.

Involvement with the Media

Television and newspapers have played a substantial role in creating awareness of the drug problem. That role has been informative, but not always positive. The media have perpetuated myths and stereotypes about addiction and its consequences. The crack baby, the junkie, and the drug pusher, as most Americans understand them, evolved from media portrayals, which often suggest that impoverished urban minorities are the only people affected by drug and alcohol abuse.

Those supporting the recovery of addicted persons and their families need to be cautious where the media are concerned, but also aware of their power and possibilities.

Above all, the confidentiality of clients and their families should be protected. Media stories about clients and their children that feature names or other identifying information should be avoided at all costs. Violations of confidentiality are usually illegal and are most certainly unethical; they are a betrayal of client trust. The media have shown a taste for the voyeuristic and sensational, and agencies must protect themselves against reporters and journalists who claim they want to tell one story, but actually tell another.

The media can, under the right circumstances, educate and promote awareness of the true nature of the addictions problem. News stories and public service spots developed with sympathetic media specialists can provide beneficial attention to the substance-abuse problem. This can best be achieved by working with a journalist or reporter who is personally known, or who has an established track record of compassionate reporting. It is crucial to retain some control over the edited material whenever possible. Spokespersons for agencies that represent families should be chosen on the basis of good impulse control and an inability to be swayed by cameras and celebrity. Those persons should be able to place focus on the positive aspects of education and human services, and should be able to answer questions calmly and succinctly under pressure. With care and attention to detail, the media can sometimes be an ally in the war against substance abuse.

In Conclusion

There are many more addictions-related issues still to be discussed; professionals from all human service fields must continue to gather together to discuss them and to develop solutions. Although born into difficult circumstances, substance-affected children often have vast reservoirs of strength. They need caring support from persons with expertise in order to overcome problems and to avoid repeating the cycle of addiction that can occur in families. Addicted parents also need support to be reminded of their personal worth, and to learn to fully participate in the lives of their children.

We hope that some of those who share our heartfelt belief that there are no throwaway adults or children will find the information in this book helpful and will be encouraged to hold fast to their faith and to go on learning.

Resources

Blechman, E.A. *Solving Child Behavior Problems at Home and at School.* Champaign, IL: Research Press, 1985.

Child Welfare: A Source Book of Knowledge and Practice. Washington, DC: Child Welfare League of America, 1985.

Cole, E., and J. Duva. *Family Preservation: An Orientation for Administrators and Practitioners.* Washington, DC: Child Welfare League of America, 1990.

Fernandez, H. *The Child Advocacy Handbook.* New York: The Pilgrim Press, 1980.

Friedman, J., et al. *Managing the Media Maze: A Resource Guide for Child Care Advocates.* Berkley, CA: Child Care Employee Project, 1984.

Garner, H.G. *Helping Others Through Teamwork.* Washington, DC: Child Welfare League of America, 1988.

Jensen, M.A., and Z.W. Chevlier. *Issues and Advocacy in Early Education.* Boston, MA: Allyn and Bacon, 1990.

Jones, C. *How to Speak TV, Print and Radio: A Self-defense Manual When You're in the News.* Tampa, FL: Video Consultants, Inc., 1991.

Larsen, J. (Ed.). *Drug Exposed Infants and Their Families: Coordinating Response of the Legal, Medical and Child Protection System. Executive Summary.* Washington, DC: American Bar Association, Center on Children and the Law, 1990.

Magura, S., and B.S. Moses. *Outcome Measures for Child Welfare Services.* Washington, DC: Child Welfare League of America, 1986.

Melton, G.B., and D.S. Hargrove. *Planning Mental Health Services for Children and Youth.* New York: Guilford Press, 1994.

Minuchin, S. *Families and Family Therapy.* Cambridge, MA: Harvard University Press, 1974.

The National Directory of Children, Youth and Families Services 1993–1994. Longmont, CO: Marion L. Peterson Publishers, 1993.

Romig, D. *Justice for Our Children.* Lexington, MA: Lexington Books, 1978.

Satir, V.J., J. Stachorviak, and H.A. Taschman. *Helping Families to Change.* Northvale, NJ: Jason Aronson, Inc., 1994.

Together We Can: A Guide for Crafting a Profamily System of Education and Human Services. Washington, DC: U.S. Department of Health and Human Services, 1993.

Weil, M., et al. *Case Management in Human Service Practice: A Systematic Approach to Mobilizing Resources for Clients.* San Francisco, CA: Jossey-Bass Publishers, 1985.

Wells, K., and D.E. Biegel (Eds.). *Family Preservation Services: Research and Evaluation.* Newbury Park, CA: Sage, 1991.

What Do You Know About the Substance Abuse Problem?

1. Drugs are primarily an urban problem.   _____

2. Men abuse drugs substantially more often than women.   _____

3. Drug addicts can generally recover after two to three months
   in a treatment program.   _____

4. Drug and alcohol treatment is usually available in prison
   for people who request it.   _____

5. If women are HIV positive and pregnant, their babies
   will generally develop AIDS.   _____

6. Children who are prenatally exposed to cocaine often
   have physical deformities and/or mental deficits.   _____

7. Marijuana is safe for use by pregnant women.   _____

8. The most widely used drug is cocaine.   _____

9. Drug use is generally triggered by teenage experimentation
   with cigarettes and alcohol.   _____

10. Parents who abuse drugs usually abuse their children.   _____

Answer Key: The answer to questions 1 through 10 is "no."

BIBLIOGRAPHY

Ackerman, R.J. (Ed.). *Growing in the Shadow: Children of Alcoholics*. Pompano Beach, FL: Health Practitioners, 1986.

Addicted Parents and Their Children: Two Reports. Rockville, MD: National Institute on Drug Abuse, 1980.

Anderson, B., and E. Novick, *Fetal Alcohol Syndrome and Pregnant Women Who Abuse Alcohol: An Overview of the Issue and the Federal Response*. Washington, DC: U.S. Department of Health and Human Services, February 1992.

Anthony, E.J., and C. Chiland (Eds.). *The Child in His Family: Perilous Development : Child Raising and Identity Formation Under Stress*. New York: John Wiley, 1988.

Bayley, N. *Manual for the Bayley Scales of Infant Development*. New York: The Psychological Corporation, 1969.

Behrman, R.E. (Ed.). *The Future of Children: Drug-Exposed Children*. Los Altos, CA: The David and Lucile Packard Foundation, 1991.

Benard, B. *Fostering Resiliency in Kids: Protective Factors in the Family, School, and Community*. Portland, OR: Western Regional Center for Drug-Free Schools and Communities, August 1991.

Beschner, G., and R.B. Rotman (Eds.). *Symposium on Comprehensive Health Care for Addicted Families and Their Children*. Washington, DC: U.S. Government Printing Office, 1977.

Bozeman, W.C. *Drug Testing in Schools: Implications for Policy*. Alexandria, VA: National School Boards Association, 1987.

Brazelton, T.B. "Neonatal Behavioral Assessment Scale, Second Edition." *Clinics in Developmental Medicine*, No. 88. Philadelphia, PA: Lippincott, 1984.

Brown, S.S. (Ed.). *Children and Parental Illicit Drug Use: Research, Clinical, and Policy Issues, Summary of a Workshop*. Washington, DC: National Academy Press, 1991.

Call, J., et al (Eds.) *Frontiers in Infant Psychiatry*. Volume II, New York: Basic Books, Inc., 1984.

Chasnoff, I.J. *A First: National Hospital Incidence Survey*. Chicago, IL: National Association for Perinatal Addiction Research and Education, 1989.

Chasnoff, I.J. *Drugs, Alcohol, Pregnancy and Parenting*. Boston, MA: Kluwer Academic Publishers, 1988.

Children at the Front: A Different View of the War on Alcohol and Drugs. New York: Child Welfare League of America, 1992.

Children Today, Special Issue on Prenatal Substance Abuse, 19(4), July/August, 1990.

Cocaine Babies: Florida's Substance-exposed Youth. Tallahassee, FL: Office of Policy, Research and Improvement.

Cook, P.S., R.C. Petersen, and D.T. Moore. *Alcohol, Tobacco, and Other Drugs May Harm the Unborn*. Rockville, MD: U.S. Department of Health and Human Services, Office for Substance Abuse Prevention, 1990.

Costello, M., and M. Costello. *A Family Support Approach in a Residential and Outpatient Chemical Dependency Center: Treatment Milieu, Parenting Programs and Structured Children's Programs*. Olympia, WA: Division of Alcohol and Substance Abuse, 1993.

Crack and Other Addictions: Old Realities and New Challenges. Washington, DC: Child Welfare League of America, 1991.

Crack Babies. Washington, DC: Department of Health and Human Services, Office of Inspector General, 1990.

Delapenha, L. *Strategies for Teaching Young Children Prenatally Exposed to Drugs*. Perinatal Addiction Research and Education Update, March 1991.

Donovan, D.M., M. Dennis, and G.A. Marlatt (Eds.). *Assessment of Addictive Behaviors*. New York: Guilford Press, 1988.

Dorris, M. *The Broken Cord*. New York: HarperCollins Publishers, 1989.

Drug Abuse Information and Referrals in the Special Supplemental Food Program for Women, Infants, and Children: A Resource Manual for Program Development. Washington, DC: U.S. Department of Agriculture, 1990.

Drug Exposed Children Aged 2 to 5: Identifying Their Needs and Planning for Early Intervention. Rockville, MD: U.S. Department of Health and Human Services, Public Health Service, Alcohol, Drug Abuse and Mental Health Administration, 1991.

Drug-Exposed Infants: A generation at risk. Washington, DC: General Accounting Office, 1990.

Drug-Exposed Infants and Their Families: Coordinating responses of the legal, medical, and child protection system. Washington, DC: American Bar Association, 1990.

Equals in This Partnership: Parents of Disabled and At-risk Infants and Toddlers Speak to Professionals. Washington, DC: National Center for Clinical Infant Programs, 1985.

Field, T., et al. (Eds.). *Infants Born at Risk: Behavior and Development*. New York: Spectrum, 1979.

Finnegan, L. (Ed.). *Drug Dependency in Pregnancy: Clinical Management of Mother and Child: A Manual for Medical Professionals and Para Professionals*. Rockville, MD: National Institute on Drug Abuse, 1987.

Galanter, M. (Ed.). *Recent Developments in Alcoholism*. Vol. 9. New York: Plenum Publishing Corporation, 1991.

Gittins, N.E. (Ed.). *Fighting Drugs in the Schools: A Legal Manual*. Alexandria, VA: National School Boards Association, 1988.

Harms, E. *Drugs and Youth: The Challenge of Today*. New York: Pergamon Press, 1973.

Hawkins, J.D., et al. *Childhood Predictors of Adolescent Substance Abuse: Toward an Empirically Grounded Theory*. New York: Haworth Press, 1986.

Healthy Mothers, Healthy Babies: A Compendium of Program Ideas for Serving Low-income Women. Washington, DC: National Maternal and Child Health Clearinghouse, 1986.

Hutchings, D.E. (Ed.). *Prenatal Abuse of Licit and Illicit Drugs*. New York: Academy of Science, 1989.

Johnson, J.L., and L.A. Bennett. *School-aged Children of Alcoholics: Theory and Research*. Piscataway, NJ: Rutgers, the State University, 1988.

Kalant, O. *Alcohol and Drug Problems in Women: Research Advances in Alcohol and Drug Problems*. Vol. 5. New York: Plenum Publishing Corporation, 1980.

Klaus, M.H., and J.H. Kennell. *Maternal-Infant Bonding*. St. Louis, MO: C.V. Mosby, 1976.

Kumpfer, K.L. *Youth at High Risk for Substance Abuse*. Rockville, MD: U.S. Department of Health and Human Services, National Institute on Drug Abuse, 1987.

Lowinson, J.H., et al. *Substance Abuse: A Comprehensive Textbook*, Second Edition. Baltimore, MD: Williams and Wilkins, 1992.

Meyers, R.E. (Ed.). *Psychopathology and Addictive Disorders*. New York: Guilford Press, 1986.

Moos, R.H. *Family Environment Scale*. Palo Alto, CA: Consulting Psychologists Press, 1974.

Morse, B.A., and L. Weiner. *FAS: Parent and Child*. Brookline, MA: Massachusettes Health Research Institute, 1992.

National Center on Child Abuse and Neglect. *Child Abuse and Neglect: A Shared Community Concern*. Washington, DC: U. S. Department of Health and Human Services, Children's Bureau, 1989.

National Center on Child Abuse and Neglect. *Study of National Incidence and Prevalence of Child Abuse and Neglect : 1988*. Washington, DC: U. S. Department of Health and Human Services, Children's Bureau, 1988.

Neibyl, J.R. (Ed.). *Drug Use in Pregnancy*. Philadelphia, PA: Lea and Febiger, 1987.

Northwest Regional Perinatal Care Program. *Substance Abuse During Pregnancy: A Resource and Information Guide for the Health Care Practitioner*. Seattle, WA: March of Dimes, Western Washington Chapter, 1990.

Office on Smoking and Health. *The Health Consequences of Smoking for Women: A Report of the Surgeon General*. Rockville, MD: The Office, 1980.

One Thousand Babies. Philadelphia, PA: Philadelphia Perinatal Society and Philadelphia Department of Health, 1989.

Petrakis, P.L. *The Fetal Alcohol Syndrome and Related Disorders*. Rockville, MD: National Institute on Alcohol Abuse and Addiction, 1987.

Pinkert, T.M. (Ed.). *Current Research on the Consequences of Maternal Drug Use*. Washington, DC: National Institute on Drug Abuse Research Series, U.S. Government Printing Office, 1985.

Randels, S. *The Needs of Families with FAS/FAE Children*. Snohomish County Health District Conference on Fetal Alcohol Syndrome and Fetal Alcohol Effects, May 1992.

Reaching Out: A Directory of National Organizations Related to Maternal and Child Health. National Maternal and Child Health Clearinghouse, 1989.

Reed, B.G., et al. *Addicted Women: Family Dynamics, Self-Perceptions and Support Systems*. Institute for Social Research at the University of Michigan, 1977.

Reed, B.G., G.M. Beschner, and J. Mondonaro (Eds.). *Treatment Services for Drug Dependent Women*. Volumes I and II. NIDA Treatment Research Monograph Series. Rockville, MD: National Institute on Drug Abuse, 1980/1982.

Rosenbaum, M. *Just Say What? An Alternative View on Solving America's Drug Problem*. National Council on Crime and Delinquency, 1989.

Sonderegger, T.B. *Perinatal Substance Abuse and Clinical Implications*. Baltimore, MD: Johns Hopkins University Press, 1992.

Spang, B.P. and Redding, J.M. *Guidelines for Setting Up Support Groups in Schools*. Augusta, ME: Maine State Department of Educational and Cultural Services, 1984.

Spitz, H.I., and J.J. Rosecam (Eds.). *Cocaine Abuse: New Directions in Treatment and Research*. New York: Brunner/Mazel, 1987.

Stump, J. *Our Best Hope: Early Intervention with Prenatally Drug-exposed Infants and Their Families*. Washington, DC: Child Welfare League of America, 1991.

Sugarman, J.M. *Building Early Childhood Systems: A Resource Handbook*. Washington, DC: Child Welfare League of America, 1991.

The Health Consequences of Involuntary Smoking: A Report of the Surgeon General. Rockville, MD: U.S. Public Health Service, 1986.

Thomas, S.B. *Health Related Legal Issues in Education*. Topeka, KS: National Organization on Legal Problems in Education, 1987.

Today's Challenge: Teaching Strategies for Working with Young Children Prenatally Exposed to Drugs/Alcohol. Pamphlet issued by Los Angeles Unified School District. Los Angeles, CA: The School District, 1989.

Towers, R.L. *Children of Alcoholics/Addicts*. Washington, DC: National Education Association, 1989.

U.S. Department of Education. *Schools Without Drugs*. Washington, DC: The Department, 1986.

U.S. Department of Health and Human Services. *Questions and Answers: Teenage Alcohol Use and Abuse*. Washington, DC: National Institute on Alcohol Abuse and Alcoholism, 1983.

U.S. Department of Justice. *Drugs of Abuse*. Washington, DC: Drug Enforcement Administration, 1988.

Villarreal, S.F., L.E. McKinney, and M. Quackenbush. *Handle with Care: Helping Children Prenatally-exposed to Drugs and Alcohol*. Santa Cruz, CA: ETR Associates, 1992.

Washton, A.M. *Cocaine Addiction: Treatment, Recovery, and Relapse Prevention*. New York: Norton, 1989.

Weiner, S. *Perinatal Impact of Substance Abuse*. White Plains, New York: March of Dimes, 1992.

Wolf, D. *Child Abuse—Implications of Child Development and Psychopathology*. Newbury Park, CA: Sage Publications, 1987.

APPENDIX A

Agencies/ Clearinghouses/ Support Groups

American Council for Drug Education
204 Monroe Street
Suite 110
Rockville, MD 20852
(301) 294-0600

American Federation of Parents for Drug-Free Youth
8730 Georgia Avenue
Suite 200
Silver Springs, MD 20910
1-800-554-KIDS

Beginning Alcohol and Addiction Basic Education (BABES)
17730 Northland Park Court
Southfield, MI 48075
(313) 443-1676
1-800-BABES

Bureau of Justice Clearinghouse
Box 6000
Rockville, MD 20850
1-800-3277

Chemical People Project
The Public Television Outreach Alliance
c/o WQED-TV
4802 Fifth Avenue
Pittsburgh, PA 15213
(412) 391-0900

Clearinghouse on Child Abuse and Neglect Information
P.O. Box 1182
Washington, DC 20013
(703) 821-2086

Clearinghouse for Drug-Exposed Children
Division of Behavioral and Developmental Pediatrics
University of California, San Francisco
400 Parnassus Avenue
Room A 203
San Francisco, CA 94143-0314
(415) 476-9691

Cocannon Family Groups
P.O. Box 64742-66
Los Angeles, CA 90064
(213) 859-2206

Drugs and Crime Data Center and Clearinghouse
Box 6000
Rockville, MD 20850
1-800-666-3332

Families Anonymous
P.O. Box 528
Van Nuys, CA 91408
(818) 989-7841

Fetal Alcohol and Drug Unit
University of Washington School of Nursing
Department of Psychiatry and Behavioral Sciences
2707 Northeast Blakeley Street
Seattle, WA 98105
(206) 543-7155

First American Prevention Center
P.O. Box 529
Bayfield, WI 54814
(715) 779-3177
1-800-643-9912

Hazelden Foundation
Pleasant Valley Road
Box 176
Center City, MN 55012-0176
1-800-328-9000

Healthy Mothers, Healthy Babies Coalition
409 12th Street. SW
Room 309
Washington, DC 20024
(202) 638-5577

Institute on Black Chemical Abuse, Inc.
2616 Nicollet Avenue
Minneapolis, MN 55408
(612) 871-7878

March of Dimes Birth Defects Foundation
1275 Mamaroneck Avenue
White Plains, NY 10605
(914) 428-7100

Mothers Against Drunk Driving (MADD)
P.O. Box 541688
Dallas, TX 75354-1688
(214) 744-6233

Nar-Anon Family Group Headquarters
World Service Office
P.O. Box 2562
Palos Verdes Peninsula, CA 90274
(213) 547-5800

Narcotics Anonymous World Service Office
P.O. Box 9999
Van Nuys, CA 91409
(818) 780-3951

National Association for Children of Alcoholics
31582 Coast Highway
Suite B
South Laguna, CA 92677
(714) 499-3889

National Association for the Education of Young Children
1834 Connecticut Avenue, NW
Washington, DC 20009-5786
(202) 232-8777
1-800-424-2460

National Association for Perinatal Addiction Research
11 E. Hubbard Street
Suite 200
Chicago, IL 60611
(312) 329-9131

National Association of State Alcohol and Drug Abuse Directors
444 North Capitol Street, NE
Washington, DC 20001
(202) 783-6868

National Black Child Development Institute
463 Rhode Island Avenue, NW
Washington, DC 20005
(202) 387-1281

National Center for Clinical Infant Programs
2000 14th Street North
Suite 380
Arlington, VA 20001
(703) 528-4300

National Center for Education in Maternal and Child Health
38th and R Streets, NW
Washington, DC 20005
(202) 625-8400

National Clearinghouse for Alcohol and Drug Information
P.O. Box 2345
Rockville, MD 20852
(301) 468-2600
1-800-729-6686

National Coalition of Hispanic Health and Human Services Organizations
1501 16th Street, NW
Washington, DC 20036
(202) 797-4343

National Council on Alcoholism and Drug Dependence, Inc.
12 West 21st Street
8th Floor
New York, NY 10010
(212) 206-6770
1-800-NCA

National Families in Action
2296 Henderson Mill Road
Suite 204
Atlanta, GA 30345
(404) 934-6364

National Federation of Parents for Drug Free Youth
9551 Big Bend
St. Louis,MO 63122
(314) 968-1322

National Head Start Association
1220 King Street
Suite 200
Arlington, VA 22314
(703) 739-0875

National Institute on Drug Abuse
Drug-Referral Helpline
5600 Fishers Lane
Rockville, MD 20857
1-800-662-HELP

National Maternal and Child Health Clearinghouse
38th and R Streets, NW
Washington, DC 20057
(202) 625-8410

National Organization on Fetal Alcohol Syndrome
1815 H Street, NW
Washington, DC 20006
(202) 785-4585

National PTA Drug and Alcohol Abuse Prevention Project
700 North Rush Street
Chicago, IL 60611
(312) 577-4500

National Sudden Infant Death Syndrome Clearinghouse
8201 Greensboro Drive
McLean, VA 22102
(703) 821-8955

Office for Substance Abuse Prevention
U.S. Department of Health and Human Services
5600 Fishers Lane
Rockville, MD 20857
(301) 443-0369

Office of Minority Health Resource Center
U.S. Department of Health and Human Services
Public Health Service
P.O. Box 37337
Washington, DC 20013-7337
1-800-444-6472

Office on Smoking and Health Technical Information Center
5600 Fishers Lane
Park Building
Room 116
Rockville, MD 20857
(301) 443-1690

Parent Resource Institute for Drug Education
(PRIDE)
100 Edgewood Avenue
Suite 1216
Atlanta, GA 30303
(404) 658-2548
1-800-241-7946

Project CODE (Collaboration on Drug Education)
Community Connections, Inc.
3516 Tony Drive
San Diego, CA 92122
(619) 453-2361

Safe Homes
P.O. Box 702
Livingston, NJ 07039

Teratology Society
9650 Rockville Pike
Bethesda, MD 20814
(301) 571-1841

Toughlove
P.O. Box 1069
Doylestown, PA 18901
(215) 348-7090
1-800-333-1069

APPENDIX B

Audiovisual Resources

A Challenge to Care: Strategies to Help Chemically Dependent Women (videotape). Cambridge, MA: Vida Health Communications, 1992.

A Conversation with Magic (videotape). Nickelodeon, 1992.

Addiction: The Problems, The Solutions (videotape). Pleasantville, NY: Sunset Communications, 1990.

America Hooked on Drugs (16mm/videotape). Deerfield, IL: MTI Film and Video, 1986.

America Hurts: The Drug Epidemic (16mm/videotape). Deerfield, IL: MTI Film and Video, 1987.

Bodywatch: No Butts (16mm/videotape). Deerfield, IL: MTI Film and Video, 1987.

Breathing Easy (videotape). Deerfield, IL: MTI Film and Video, 1984.

Coke Isn't It: Hard Facts About Cocaine (videotape). Mt. Kisko, NY: Guidance Associates, 1989.

Drug Free Me (videotape). New York: Select Media, 1990.

Honour of All (videotape about impact of alcohol abuse). Issaquah, WA: Phil Lucas Productions, Inc., 1985.

Hugs Invited: An Educational Training Series (videotape series for human service workers serving children/families with HIV/AIDS). Washington, DC: Child Welfare League of America, 1991.

Inhalant Abuse: Kids in Danger/Adults in the Dark (videotape). Dallas, TX: Media Projects, Inc., 1990.

Kids Talking to Kids (videotape). New York: Children of Alcoholics Foundation, Inc., 1989.

Little, R.E., "Pregnancy and the Fetal Alcohol Syndrome" (slide show), Unit 5 of *Alcohol Use and Its Medical Consequences: A Comprehensive Teaching Program for Biomedical Evaluation.* Project of Dartmouth Medical School, 1982.

One for My Baby (16mm film). Madison, WI: Friends of WHA Television, 1982.

Pregnancy on the Rocks: The Fetal Alcohol Syndrome (16mm film). Coronado, CA: Peter Glaws Productions, 1982.

Sex, Drugs and AIDS (videotape). ODN Productions, 1987.

Steroids: Shortcut to Make-believe Muscles (videotape). Pleasantville, NY: Sunburst Communications, 1990.

Straight from the Heart: Stories of Mothers Recovering from Addiction (videotape). Cambridge, MA: Vida Health Communications, 1992.

Teaching Healthy Choices: Strategies for Substance Abuse Prevention in Grades K–12 (videotape). New York: Select Media, 1990.

The Substance Abuse Series (six videotapes on drug/alcohol abuse prevention). South Deerfield, MA: Channing L. Bete Company, Inc., 1990.

Too Little, Too Late (videotape featuring families with loved ones who died of AIDS). Fanlight Productions, 1988.

Wasted: A True Story (16mm/videotape). Deerfield, IL: MTI Film and Video, 1983.

When Your Parent Drinks Too Much (16mm/videotape). Deerfield, IL: MTI Film and Video, 1987.

With Loving Arms (videotape depicting foster families caring for children with AIDS). Washington, DC: Child Welfare League of America, 1989.

Women, Drugs and Alcohol (16mm/videotape). Deerfield, IL: MTI Film and Video, 1980.

APPENDIX C

Journals and Periodicals on Substance Abuse

ADAHM News
Department of Health and Human Services
Alcohol, Drug Abuse, and Mental Health Association
Parklawn Building
Room 12C-15
5600 Fishers Lane
Rockville, MD 20857
(301) 443-3783

Addictions Alert
American Health Consultants
Six Piedmont Center
3525 Piedmont Road, NE
Suite 400
Atlanta, GA 30305
(404) 262-7436

Addictive Behaviors
Pergamon Press, Inc.
Journals Division
Maxwell House
Fairview Park
Elmsford, NY 10523
(914) 592-7700

Addictive Programs Management
American Health Consultants
Six Piedmont Center
3525 Piedmont Road, NE
Suite 400
Atlanta, GA 30305
(404) 262-7436

ADPA Professional
Alcohol and Drug Problems Association of North America
444 N. Capitol Street, NW
Suite 706
Washington, DC 20001
(202) 737-4340

AID Bulletin
Addictions Intervention with the Disabled
Project AID
c/o Sociology Department
Lawry Hall
Kent State University
Kent, OH 44242
(216) 672-2440

Alcohol and Alcoholism
Pergamon Press, Inc.
Journals Division
Maxwell House
Fairview Park
Elmsford, NY 10523
(914) 592-7700

Alcohol and Drug Abuse PULSE BEATS Newsletter
4325 Sheperdsville Road
Box 18630
Lewisville, KY 40218
(502) 459-7910

Alcohol Clinical Update
Project Cork Institute
Dartmouth Medical School
Hanover, MA 03756
(603) 646-7540

Alcohol-Codependency-Addictions Lifeline
Foundation for Alcoholism Communication
352 Halladay Street
Seattle, WA 98109
1-800-543-3596

Alcohol Health and Research World
U.S. National Institute on Alcohol Abuse and Alcoholism
1400 Eye Street, N.W.
Suite 600
Washington, DC 20402
(202) 842-7600

Alcohol Recovery Services: Directory of Community Resources in California
Department of Alcohol and Drug Problems
1700 K Street
Sacramento, CA 95814-4022
(916) 323-2014

Alcoholism and Addictions Magazine
IPG 4959 Commerce Parkway
Cleveland, OH 44128
1-800-342-6237

Alcoholism Briefs
DelMar Publications
1165 Elmwood Place
Deerfield, IL 60015

Alcoholism: Clinical and Experimental Research
Research Society on Alcoholism
Williams and Wilkins
428 E. Preston Street
Baltimore, MD 21202
(301) 528-4000

Alcoholism Treatment Quarterly
Haworth Press
10 Alice Street
Binghamton, NY 13904
1-800-342-9678

American Journal of Drug and Alcohol Abuse
Marcel Dekker Journals
270 Madison Avenue
New York, NY 10016
(212) 696-9000

Annual Review of Addicions Research and Treatment
Pergamon Press, Inc.
Journals Division
Maxwell House
Fairview Park
Elmsford, NY 10523
(914) 592-7700

Bulletin on Narcotics
United Nations Publications
Room DC2-853
New York, NY 10017
(212) 963-8300

CA-DE News
Council for Alcohol and Drug Education of New Jersey
526 Route 206
Trenton, NJ 08610
(609) 291-0500

Chemical Dependency
Greenhaven Press, Inc.
Box 289009
San Diego, CA 92198-0009
(619) 485-7424

Contemporary Drug Problems
Federal Legal Publications, Inc.
157 Chambers Street
New York, NY 10007
(212) 619-4949

Controlled Substance Handbook
Government Information Services
1611 N. Kent Street
Suite 508
Arlington, VA 22209
(703) 528-1000

Coping Catalog
Washington Area Council on Alcohol and Drug Abuse, Inc.
1232 M Street, NW
Washington, DC 20005
(202) 783-1300

Drug and Alcohol Dependence
Elsevier Science, Inc.
Box 882
Madison Square Station
New York, NY 10159
(212) 989-5800

Drug Law Report
Clark Boardman Company, LTD.
435 Hudson Street
New York, NY 10014
(212) 929-7500

Drugs and Drug Abuse Newsletter
Editorial Resources, Inc.
Box 21133
Washington, DC 20009
(206) 322-8387

Drugs and Society
Haworth Press
10 Alice Street
Binghamton, NY 13904
1-800-342-9678

Drugs in the Workplace
Business Research Publications, Inc.
817 Broadway
Third Floor
New York, NY 10003
(212) 673-4700

EAP Digest Employee Assistance Programs
Performance Resource Press
2145 Crooks Road
Troy, MI 48084
(313) 643-9580

Focus—Education Professionals and Family Recovery
U.S. Journal, Inc.
3201 W. 15th Street
Deerfield, Beach, FL 33442

Guide to Federal Funding for Anti-Drug Programs
Government Information Services
1611 N. Kent Street
Suite 508
Arlington, VA 22209
(703) 528-1000

Health Consequences of Smoking
U.S. Office of Smoking and Health
Centers for Disease Control
Technical Information Center
Park Building
Room 116
5600 Fishers Lane
Rockville, MD 20857
(301) 443-1575

ICPA Quarterly
International Commission for Prevention of
Alcoholism and Drug Dependency
6830 Laurel Street, NW
Washington, DC 20012
(202) 722-6729

Interdisciplinary Studies in Alcohol Use and Abuse
Edwin Mellen Press
240 Portage Road
Box 450
Lewiston, NY 14097
(716) 754-8566

International Journal of the Addictions
Marcel Dekker Journals
270 Madison Avenue
New York, NY 10016
(212) 696-9000

Journal of Adolescent Chemical Dependency
Haworth Press
10 Alice Street
Binghamton, NY 13904
1-800-342-9678

Journal of Alcohol and Drug Education
Alcohol and Drug Problems Association of North America
c/o MICAP
Box 10212
Lansing, MI 48901

Journal of Alcohol, Drugs, and Other Psychotropic Substances
Box 517
Berwyn, PA 19312
(610) 644-4944

Journal of Chemical Dependency Treatment
Haworth Press
10 Alice Street
Binghamton, NY 13904
1-800-342-9678

Journal of Child and Adolescent Substance Abuse
Haworth Press
10 Alice Street
Binghamton, NY 13904
1-800-342-9678

Journal of Drug Education
Baywood Publishing Company, Inc.
26 Austin Avenue
Box 337
Amityville, NY 11701
(516) 691-1270

Journal of Drug Issues
Journal of Drug Issues, Inc.
Box 4021
Tallahassee, FL 32303

Journal of Maintenance in the Addictions
Haworth Press
10 Alice Street
Binghamton, NY 13904
1-800-342-9678

Journal of Psychoactive Drugs
Haight-Ashbury Publications
409 Clayton Street
Second Floor
San Francisco, CA 94117
(415) 365-1904

Journal of Studies on Alcohol
Rutgers Center of Alcohol Studies
Publications Division
Box 969
Piscataway, NJ 08855
(908) 932-2190

Journal of Substance Abuse
Ablex Publishing Corporation
355 Chestnut Street
Norwood, NJ 07648
(201) 767-8450

Journal of Substance Abuse Treatment
North Shore University Hospital
Pergamon Press, Inc.
Journals Division
Maxwell House
Fairview Park
Elmsford, NY 10523
(914) 592-7700

LISTEN (Narcotics Education, Inc.)
Pacific Press Publishing Association
1350 Kings Road
Nampa, ID 38651
(208) 465-2500

National Report on Substance Abuse
Buraff Publications
1350 Connecticut Avenue, NW
Suite 1000
Washington, DC 20036
1-800-333-1291

Neurotoxicology and Teratology
Elsevier Science, Ltd.
600 White Plains Road
Tarrytown, NY 10591-5153
(914) 524-9200

Nursing Drug Alert
Michael J. Powers and Company
374 Millburn Avenue
Millburn, NJ 07041

Psychology of Addictive Behaviors
American Psychological Association
1200 17th Street, NW
Washington, DC 20036
(202) 336-5600

Women's Recovery Network
WebWorld Press, Inc.
Box 141554
Columbus, OH 43214
(614) 267-3698

APPENDIX D

Materials for Drug and Alcohol Education

BOOKS

Ackerman, R. *Children of Alcoholics: A Guidebook for Parents, Educators, and Therapists*. New York: Simon and Schuster, 1983.

A Little More About Alcohol. Lansing, MI: Alcohol Research Information Service, 1984.

Andrews, M. *The Parents' Guide to Drugs*. New York: Doubleday, 1972.

Bennett, W.J. *What Works: Schools Without Drugs*. Washington, DC: U.S. Department of Education, 1986.

Buckhalt, J.A., et al. *Rural Drug Abuse Prevention: Establishing Needs and Implementing Programs*. Presented at the annual meeting of the American Psychological Association, Boston, MA, August 1990.

California Department of Justice. *Drugs and Youth: An Information Guide for Parents and Educators*. Crime Prevention Center of the Office of the Attorney General and the Bureau of Narcotics Enforcement, 1988.

California State Office of the Attorney General. *Schools and Drugs: A Guide to Drug and Alcohol Abuse Prevention Curricula and Programs*. Revised Edition. Sacramento, CA: The Office, 1991.

Carter, S., and U.J. Oyemade. *Children Getting a Head Start Against Drugs*. Washington, DC: U.S. Department of Health and Human Services, National Head Start Association, 1993.

Carter, S., and U.J. Oyemade. *Children Getting a Head Start Against Drugs, Teacher's Guide*. Washington, DC: U.S. Department of Health and Human Services, National Head Start Association, 1993.

Carter, S., and U.J. Oyemade. *Parents Getting a Head Start Against Drugs*. Washington, DC: U.S. Department of Health and Human Services, National Head Start Association, 1993.

Carter, S., and U.J. Oyemade. *Parents Getting a Head Start Against Drugs, Trainer's Guide*. Washington, DC: U.S. Department of Health and Human Services, National Head Start Association, 1993.

Chew or Snuff Is Real Bad Stuff. Bethesda, MD: National Cancer Institute, U.S. Department of Health and Human Services.

Christy's Chance. Santa Cruz, CA: Network Publications, 1987.

Colman, W. *Understanding and Preventing AIDS*. Childrens' Press, 1988.

Cosby, W., and J. Willoughby. *Buzzy's Rebound.* Rockville, MD: National Clearinghouse for Alcohol and Drug Information, 1986.

Different Like Me: A Book for Teens Who Worry About Their Parents' Use of Alcohol/Drugs. Minneapolis, MN: Johnson Institute, 1987.

Donohue, L., H.E. Sypher, and W.J. Bukoski (Eds.). *Persuasive Communication and Drug Abuse Prevention.* Hillsdale, NJ: Lawrence Erlbaum Associates, 1991.

Don't Lose a Friend to Drugs. Washington, DC: National Crime Prevention Council, 1986.

English, J., et al. *Drug Education Through Literature: An Annotated Bibliography for Grades K–6.* Portland, OR: Western Regional Center for Drug-Free Schools and Communities, 1991.

English, J., et al. *Drug Education through Literature: An Annotated Bibliography for Grades 7–12.* Portland, OR: Western Regional Center for Drug-Free Schools and Communities, 1991.

Ertle, V., and R.M. Gabriel. *Sharing Your Success: Summaries of Successful Programs and Strategies Supporting Drug-Free Schools and Communities.* Portland, OR: Western Regional Center for Drug-Free Schools and Communities, 1991.

Flatter, C.H., and K. McCormick. *Learning to Live Drug Free: A Curriculum Model for Prevention.* Washington, DC: U.S. Department of Education, 1989.

Girdano, D.A., and D.D. Girdano. *Drug Education: Content and Methods.* Reading, MA: Addison-Wesley, 1976.

Growing Up Drug Free: A Parent's Guide to Prevention. Washington, DC: U.S. Department of Education, 1992.

Henry, G. *Purple Turtles Say No, No to Drugs.* Edmonds, WA: Purple Turtle Books, Inc.

Hyppo, M.H., and J.M. Hastiger. *An Elephant in the Living Room: The Children's Book.* Minneapolis, MN: CompCare Publications, 1984.

Lewis, J.F., et al. *Drug and Alcohol Abuse in Schools: A Practical Guide for Administrators and Teachers on How to Combat Drugs and Alcohol.* Topeka, KS: National Organization on Legal Problems of Education, 1987.

Linney, J.A., et al. *Evaluating Alcohol and Other Drug Prevention Programs at the School and Community Level.* Southeast Regional Center for Drug Free Schools and Communities, 1989.

Mann, P. *The Sad Story of Mary Wanna or How Marijuana Harms You.* New York: Woodmere Press, 1988.

National Association of Secondary School Principals. *Drug Prevention Programs— Strong Policies, Strong Actions.* NASSP Curriculum Report 17: 5, 1–6. Reston, VA: NASSP, April 1988.

New Jersey State Department of Education. *Chemical Health Education Resources.* Trenton, NJ: The Department, 1990.

North Carolina State Department of Justice. *Drug Abuse Resistance Education (D.A.R.E.). Administrative Orientation.* Revised. Raleigh, NC: The Department, 1990.

North Carolina State Department of Justice. *Drug Abuse Resistance Education (D.A.R.E.). Faculty Orientation.* Raleigh, NC: The Department, 1990.

Office of Educational Research and Improvement. *Profiles of Successful Drug Prevention Programs, 1988–1989. Drug Free School Recognition Program.* Washington, DC: The Office, 1990.

Parenting as Prevention: Preventing Alcohol and Other Drug Use Problems in the Family. Washington, DC: U.S. Department of Health and Human Services, Office of Substance Abuse Prevention, 1989.

Perkins, W.M., and N. McMurtrie-Perkins. *Raising Drug-Free Kids in a Drug-Filled World.* Center City, MN: Hazelden, 1986.

Quackenbush, M., and S.F. Villarreal. *Does AIDS Hurt? Educating Young Children About AIDS*, Second Edition, CA: ETR Associates, 1992.

Rattray, J., et al. *Kids and Alcohol: Get High on Life.* Pompano Beach, FL: Health Communications, Inc., 1984.

Schroeder, B. *Help Kids Say NO to Drugs and Drinking: A Practical Prevention Guide for Parents.* Alcoholism Council of Nebraska, 1987.

Schwandt, M.K. *Kooch Talks About Alcoholism.* Fargo, ND: Serenity Work, 1984.

Scott, S. *Peer Pressure Reversal.* Amherst, MA: Human Resource Development Press, 1985.

Seixas, J. *Alcohol: What It Is, What It Does.* New York: Greenwillow Books, 1977.

Taylor, C. *The House that Crack Built.* San Francisco: Chronicle Books, 1992.

Ten Steps to Help Your Child Say "No:" A Parents' Guide. Rockville, MD: National Clearinghouse for Alcohol and Drug Information, 1986.

The Fact Is . . . You Can Prevent Alcohol and Other Drug Problems Among Elementary School Children. Rockville, MD: National Clearinghouse for Alcohol and Drug Information, 1988.

The Fact Is . . . You Can Prevent Alcohol and Other Drug Problems Among Secondary School Students. Rockville, MD: National Clearinghouse for Alcohol and Drug Information, 1988.

Tobias, J. *Kids and Drugs: A Handbook for Parents and Professionals.* Annandale, VA: PANDAA Press, 1987.

University of Maryland. *Model University Program for Education and Prevention of Drug Abuse, Recommendations of the Task Force on Drug Policies, Enforcement, and Education, University of Maryland.* College Park, MD: The University, 1986.

Western Center for Drug-Free Schools and Communities: *A Guide to Expanding School-Based Prevention.* Portland, OR: Northwest Regional Laboratory, 1989.

Whiskers Says No to Drugs. Middletown, CT: Weekly Reader Skills Books. Field Publications, 1987.

Youcha, G., and J.S. Seixas. *Drugs, Alcohol, and Your Children: How to Keep Your Family Substance Free.* New York: Crown Publishers, 1989.

Young Children and Drugs: What Parents Can Do. Madison, WI: The Wisconsin Clearinghouse, 1987.

SUBSTANCE-ABUSE CURRICULA

Alvy, K.T., and M. Marigna. *Effective Black Parenting Program* (Curriculum for black parenting skills development). Studio City, CA: Center for the Improvement of Child Caring, 1985.

BABES (Curriculum for preschool and primary age children promoting self-esteem and decision making using puppets and stories). Southfield, MI: BABESWORLD Home, 1-800-54-BABES.

Begin Early (Curriculum, videotape, parent-child activities for children under age 5). Troy, NY: Substance Abuse Prevention Education Program, (518) 270-2800.

Breighner, K., and D. Roke. *I Am Amazing: A Program Promoting Health, Safety and Self-Esteem* (Curriculum for young children on health, safety and self-esteem), Circle Pines, MN: American Guidance Service, 1990, 1-800-328-2650.

Common Sense: Strategies for Raising Alcohol- and Drug-Free Children. National PTA and GTE Corporation, 1-800-225-5483.

Discovering Normal: A Parenting Program for Adult Children of Alcoholics and Their Partners (6 to 10 week course for parents who are adult children of alcoholics). New York: Children of Alcoholics Foundation, Inc., (212) 754-0656.

Evans, D.W., and S. Giarratano. *Into Adolescence: Avoiding Drugs* (Curriculum for grades 5-8, includes student workbook and teacher's guide), Menlo Park, CA: Walter S. Johnson Foundation, 1990.

Families and Schools Together (FAST) (Designed to assist children from preschool through middle-school age and their families considered at risk for later problems, including substance abuse). Madison, WI: FAST/Family Service, (608) 251-7611.

Families for Prevention (Videotape for parents of third graders to view at home, includes 20 question test to assess child's risk of later substance abuse). Omaha, NB: Experience Education, 1-800-477-4236.

Families in Touch (Six-book series on alcohol, drugs, sex, and AIDS for parents and their children ages 5–15 years). Evanston, IL: The Parents in Touch Project, 1-800-864-5660.

Fatal Addiction: The Selling of Addiction (Understanding the role of the media in influencing addiction, uses articles and action ideas). Los Angeles, CA: Center for Media and Values, (213) 559-2944.

Feelings, Body Changes, and Stress (Uses puppets, video to help relieve preschool children's stress and to provide parent education). Atlanta, GA: Pre-School Stress Relief Project, (404) 344-2021.

First American Prevention Center. *Community-Based Prevention Training Curriculum* (Curriculum for preventing drug and alcohol abuse with Native American perspective). Bayfield, WI: FAPC, 1990, 1-800-634-9912.

First American Prevention Center. *Family-Oriented Home Wellness Kit* (Forty activities to strengthen Native American families and members, for preschoolers to adults). Bayfield, WI: FAPC, 1990, 1-800-634-9912.

Growing Up Strong (GUS) (Curriculum designed to build good mental health in preschool/elementary children, promote family involvement and productive home-school relations; uses dolls, puppets, role play). Norman, OK: The University of Oklahoma, Center for Child and Family Development, (405) 325-1446.

Hawkins, J.D., et al. *Preparing for the Drug Free Years* (For parents of children in grades 4–7). Seattle, WA: Developmental Research and Programs, Inc., 1-800-736-2630.

Institute for Mental Health Initiatives. *Channeling Parents' Anger* (Curriculum to help parents deal appropriately with anger). Champaign, IL: The Institute, 1992, (202) 364-7111.

It's Elementary (Uses Marvel comic books and posters to teach alcohol abuse prevention). South Laguna, CA: National Association for Children of Alcoholics, (714) 499-3889.

Konlyn, P. *Real Facts—The Truth About Drugs* (A comprehensive workshop for drug and alcohol abuse prevention). Baltimore, MD: Media Materials, Inc., 1989, (410) 633-0730.

Monahan, M.A. *I Was Always Too Busy, Am I Too Late? A Parental Plea* (Program to increase parent involvement in drug prevention), (no publisher given), 1991.

National Highway Traffic Safety Administration. *The Best Prevention: Model Alcohol and Drug Education Program*. Washington, DC: The Administration, 1984.

On Appleby's Pond (Curriculum for drug and alcohol and violence prevention for preschool and primary grades, uses puppets). Mercer, PA: Mercer County Drug and Alcohol Commission, Inc., (412) 662-1550.

Project Star (Teaches students to recognize factors that influence drug/alcohol abuse and develops skills to resist influences). Kansas City, MO: Ewing Marion Kauffman Foundation, (816) 966-3606.

Selling Addiction: A Workshop on Tobacco and Alcohol Advertising (Curriculum resource with videotape, lesson plans, handouts). Los Angeles, CA: Center for Media and Values, (213) 559-2944.

Star Parents: Skills for Effective Parenting.(Building strong home-school relationships, helping students develop healthy lifestyles and decision-making skills). Palatine, IL: IRI/Starlight Publishing, 1-800-922-9474.

Talking with Your Kids About Alcohol. (Designed to help parents know what to say to their children about alcohol). Lexington, KY: Prevention Research Institute, (606) 254-9489.

United States Department of Education. *Ombudsman: A School-Based Semester-Long Drug Education/Primary Prevention Program* (For students in grades 5 and 6). Longmont, Co: Sopris West Inc., 1992.

United States Department of Education. *ME-ME Drug and Alcohol Prevention Education Program* (For students in grades 1–6, a multidisciplinary program to raise self-esteem and avoid substance abuse). Longmont, CO: Sopris West Inc., 1992.

United States Department of Education. *The New Mode Me: Curriculum for Meeting Modern Problems*, Second Edition (Designed for secondary school students to help understand the causes and consequences of behavior). Longmont, Co: Sopris West Inc., 1992.